One Man's Improbable Pathway from
Living Straight to Loving Gay

MIKE MALONEY

CHOOSING TO BE GAY. Copyright © 2020 by Mike Maloney. All rights reserved. Printed in the United States of America. No part of this book may be used or reproduced in any manner whatsoever without written permission except in the case of brief quotations embodied in critical articles and reviews.

Library of Congress Cataloging-in-Publication data has been applied for.

ISBN 978-1-7353121-1-8

To my Family—My Former Wife and My Sons

*For a loving kindness and understanding
I can never repay.*

&

To Bon-Bon

Because I need you, to really be me.

CONTENTS

ABOUT THE TITLE: *Choosing To Be Gay*	1
COMING OUT WITHIN	5
STARTING TO THINK STRAIGHT—ABOUT COMING OUT	19
THE THAI ATTRACTION	29
INTERPRETING THE THAI ATTRACTION	45
TO BE (GAY), OR NOT TO BE	59
TAKING CARE	71
TRUTH, AND CONSEQUENCES	89
FUTURE BOY	101
THE LIGHT TOUCH	117
THE RIGHT CHOICE	129
AFTERWORD	145

Peace comes from within. Do not seek it without.
—BUDDHA

We dance round in a ring and suppose.
But the Secret sits in the middle and knows.
—ROBERT FROST

ABOUT THE TITLE:
Choosing To Be Gay

The title I've chosen is conspicuously provocative—or somewhat, at least. At its most literal level, the title, or more precisely the subtitle, is purely an honest admission: *One Man's Improbable Path from Living Straight to Loving Gay.* So, what sits before you is simply the candid retelling of a personal decision process, albeit not a particularly easy one to live through nor, for that matter, to eventually be happy about.

On another level, the title is an obvious play on the often hotly debated socio-religious question, "Is coming out gay a function of predetermined biology (e.g., some DNA factor), or merely a function of one's lifestyle choice?" Let me level with you right up front: what you are about to read will neither prove nor disprove either of these viewpoints. For one thing, as of the time of this writing, I don't believe there is any new scientific or biological evidence of a missing link "gay gene." Nor am I aware of any equally convincing evidence that living as a gay man is clearly a lifestyle alternative one gloms onto, like one might as a cultist in a commune. Quite the contrary, it seems that any and all gay lifestyle "cure" programs—whether sponsored under various religious auspices or community ones—end in abject failure. This suggests, at the very least, that there is more to being gay than merely experimenting with some whimsical or misguided alternative lifestyle from which one might be rescued.

So, I make no attempt to argue for either of these two prevalent beliefs about coming out and living one's life as a gay person. But what I do argue for is that, in fact, there **is** a choice to be made by every guy, regardless of his age or family situation, who musters the courage to come out and live as a gay male. This choice is fundamental and damn hard to grapple with, let alone to finally make. To choose to accept the truth about who you *really* are, and then to live that way comfortably, proudly even. This choice supersedes any other real or make-believe ones. When I say "supersedes," what I mean is that this is THE only choice that really matters. Simply because, for the person making it, it's the singular life choice that takes inordinate self-confidence, along with unconditional faith—yes, and hope—in everyone else's understanding and acceptance.

Believing this as I do, my utmost hope would be that anyone choosing to read on about my own story would set aside all noise from pulpits, conservative radio broadcasts, and assorted gay-bashers. Instead, try to understand, and to appreciate, what makes one's choice to accept his gayness such a high hill to climb. There are hundreds of reasons to disbelieve, deny, and interminably delay this choice—from being conditioned to believe one is damned, to believing oneself a deviant, to simply feeling one is hopelessly different from everyone else. The more all of us—straight and gay alike—can perceive and empathize with this choice, the more we can all admire and, most importantly, love those with the strength to make it for themselves.

COMING OUT WITHIN

*"Well, I've found that most guys get
here about as fast as they can."*

I'm fifty-one or two, standing alone and staring, before the master bath mirror. I'm not about to shave, brush my teeth, nor even sigh yet again over the not-so-fine lines that appear deeper daily. I just watch, needing to be sure of the one to whom I'm about to speak. Seconds tick by, maybe even a minute. And then, I hear myself speaking and see my mouth forming the words in my reflection: "Admit it. You're gay." Notice I use the pronoun "you," some final, subtle attempt at denial or at placing the blame on another, but not me . . . not "I." A few more seconds tick by until I first notice it in my eyes: these eyes aren't lying, not denying. I see that clearly. Almost imperceptibly, I detect a slight but definite slumping of my shoulders, but it's a relaxing slump, a good feeling slump. Some weight is being lifted, some very heavy weight. And then it forms at the corners of my mouth—the beginnings of a thin smile.

Counselors who are helping orientation-struggling guys accept and then openly admit their gayness usually get this principle out right up front, at the start of their counseling: *Before you can come out to others, you must first come out within.* When I heard it for the first time, it instantly made sense. How can I expect anyone else to accept what I have not yet accepted myself? And yet, as common sensible as the principle sounds, it remains a deceptively elusive one to put into practice—for me, and I've been told, others as well. Why *has* it taken so long (I'm over fifty, for Christ's sake)? I pose this obvious, and undoubtedly familiar question, to the man seated across me. With the near twenty years of experience he has had helping people like me, he gives me his best, most honest answer: "Well, I've found that most guys get here about as fast as they can."

I love this answer. It says that my coming-out-within timing is neither right nor wrong, nor more importantly, is it in any way too late. In short, anytime will do. And this take-your-time permission jibes with another saying I've read somewhere and have always found reassuring: "It takes a lifetime to become the person you want to be." What's fifty years, even if a big one, but a portion of my lifetime? And yet, the questions linger still: How could I have missed the signals along the way? More candidly, what conscious (or unconscious) delusions did I contrive—as a kind of self-defense—to evade and escape the truth?

Flashback six months or so, before my face-off with the likeness in the mirror, and two connected events from back then start to resemble not so much delusion as outright deception. The catalyst, the first event, is significant. Of all places, I'm in Kuala Lumpur, Malaysia for work. I say "of all places" because, ironically, Malaysia remains one of the least gay-accepting places on earth (not far behind Indonesia, Iran, and Uganda). But central KL houses a Western-leaning, almost-anything-goes "free zone" of sorts. One that is decidedly geared to attract international business types with its clusters of 5-Star hotels, Rodeo Road shops, and Fogo de Chao like restaurants, all within walking distance of the one-time wonder of Malaysia—the conjoined Petronas Towers. In this free zone, many goods and services are more readily available than in any other parts of the city or country. Including, naturally, services of the escort kind, both female and male.

His name is Vincent. His online profile says he is half Thai and half Malay; but it's the Thai half that piques my interest. From the first moments I spent in Bangkok a few years back, I have this sixth sense attraction to Thai guys. Though I try often to understand it, nothing I come up with helps me explain this odd, almost innate attraction. It's only one day, some years later, when my American colleague living in Bangkok remarks—as a casual but intended compliment to me—"You must have been Thai in a previous life" that anything close to a credible explanation for my magnetic attraction to Thais dawns upon me. Some email negotiations follow, but it's soon agreed that Vincent will meet me at my KL hotel room tomorrow evening. The idea isn't to be escorted out for a night in the town. It's to get to know each other more comfortably, and see what develops. Vincent's brief profile also mentions that he is a part-time masseur.

Right on time, Vincent gently knocks on my door. As is so typical with Thai's—both men and women—it's his warm, innocently eager smile that strikes my first impression of this young rather good-looking guy. He's about 22, and, as noted, is at once living up to the longstanding Travel Thailand ads, "Thailand: The Land of Smiles." Oh yes, and given his high-cheek-boned, silk-smooth skin face and jet-black hair, I have absolutely no doubts about his part-Thai heritage. As we introduce ourselves though, had I expected things to be awkward—considering this is my very first time in a situation like this—I find, on quite the contrary, that I'm completely at ease. Dare I say, never more so? This tells me something. But what happens next goes beyond telling me something—to making me *feel* something. Something that, all at once, *feels* perfectly natural and definitely self-revealing.

In lieu of sitting, talking, and sharing a mini-bar beer, Vincent asks me politely—almost shyly—if I would like a massage, as an easy way for us to get to know one another. I don't need time to think over his suggestion. It has been on my mind from the moment I read his online profile. But having never experienced a body massage by another guy, and being normally super-shy myself (to the point of being, at times, overly self-effacing), you might think I would stammer in reply with legs nervously but lightly shaking. But no. I simply smile back, drop my T-shirt and boxers, and without saying a word, lie face down naked on the bed. As I glance back over my shoulder, I see that Vincent has dropped all his clothes too.

Never, other than in large high school locker rooms, had I been naked with other boys or men, let alone with just one other guy. Yet, my only thoughts lying there were "I can't believe how unbelievably comfortable I am right now, how naturally 'normal' this all feels." At the risk of over-dramatizing, I clearly hear the words going through my mind: "I must be where I belong, with another really likable gay guy. God, just being with him feels good. This is who I am." But, as wonderful as life was feeling, I would in short order begin talking myself out of these liberating thoughts and exhilarating feelings.

This is that catalyst, or better yet, that "catalytic moment" I was referring to. A moment that both blared the truth of who I am to me and—in my virtually immediate, abject rejection of its significance—denied that truth, rationalizing that the moment meant nothing more than a one-off aberration. One that absolutely would never happen again. A most paradoxical "this is who I am, no this cannot possibly be who I am." For no sooner does Vincent sweetly kiss me goodbye and leave, that a tidal wave of sinful guilt—familiar from twelve years of elementary and secondary Catholic-nun schooling—takes over. And, of course, I do what I've been conditioned to do: start hating myself.

What's a Catholic-raised boy—even one who as an adult is, at best, more of a part-time practicing Catholic—to do? How do I start offloading at least some of this guilt? Consider the options occurring to me. Let some time pass and just try to forget all about it; get it off my chest, talk to someone; pray for forgiveness (and the willpower to never let it happen again). And one other, a real outlier for sure, go to Confession. It takes me no more than a few minutes to reject the "forget about it" option. This intimate time with someone gentle, nice, cool, and comfortably gay is too much an epiphany to ever forget. As for talking with someone to "let it all out," while that sounds potentially helpful, the question it begs makes it instantly impractical: talk with whom? Perhaps at that moment I do then turn to prayer—honestly, I don't remember. But from somewhere, I come upon a sort of inspired combo-option: maybe there is someone with whom I could speak. Someone who would likely listen unconditionally, and without me in the revealing being fearful of revelation. Someone, even (could it really be?), who might offer some small measure of forgiveness to me. Ahhh. That would be a priest—administering the Sacrament of Confession.

I've had the privilege of becoming friends with just a couple of Catholic priests in my life. First, as president of the Newman Club on campus during university days with our Newman Chaplain. Second, much later, as a daily 6 a.m. mass-goer at my neighborhood parish church, where that first Mass of the day was always celebrated by the pastor. Both men shared something in common that appealed greatly to me: when they spoke—during more formal Sunday sermons and especially during more casual daily, short ones—their thought-provoking words could almost always be turned into life-helpful actions. So stimulating were my pastor's awakening words, in fact, that on many weekdays, I would leave the thirty-minute 6 a.m. Mass thinking I had once again downed a double espresso for the soul. But at this point in my life, it has been a long while since I've formed any priestly friendships.

There is someone though, who, out of nowhere, crosses my mind. He's an Assistant Pastor at the university's Catholic parish, where I've at least attempted to reconnect with my Catholic yesteryears. In deciding to register in the parish (as evidenced quite soon thereafter by the ever-dependable weekly donation envelopes that showed up in my mail), my thinking went like this: if you're seeking a more up-to-date, even slightly more open-minded version of Catholicism today—along with, importantly, a priest staff geared to engage a younger, educated congregation with relevance—where more likely a place than at an on-campus parish? Fortunately, amongst this parish staff is one Father Tom. I've never met him, but I have attended several masses in which he was the celebrant, and in which his sermons grabbed me by the collar and wouldn't let go. Another one of those instantly captivating, though rare, double espresso preachers. And I should mention that along with his always sobering "wake-up" content, his sermons also came with a booming baritone delivery and, best of all, a most approachable, self-deprecating sense of humor. Oh yes, and one other thing that's definitely reassuring: Father Tom hasn't been shy in speaking about his past bouts with alcoholism. Though I've never met him, I feel certain I could trust him. An avowed sinner always has a better go with another avowed sinner.

Not long back from my business trip to Malaysia, then, I place a call to the parish office secretary to request an appointment to meet with Father Tom. I cannot recall ever having made an appointment for a private counseling session with a priest, so I assume it may be awhile before I hear back regarding Father Tom's availability. Imagine my surprise when, within only thirty minutes of my booking call, Father Tom himself calls me back. He asks if I am free right now. A bit caught off guard by his sudden availability, I stammer, "Yes, sure . . . but . . . but I didn't expect to hear from you so quickly." To which he replies, "When I get calls like yours—out of the blue—from someone in the parish I've yet to meet, I've learned that that someone is likely in real need of help, sooner rather than later. How soon can you get to the parish office?"

But there is more behind my stammered response than the jolt of Father Tom's sudden callback. The guilt bag I'm lugging around is a doubly loaded one: it's not just that I've engaged in gay sex, I've done it as a married man. Taken together, these two transgressions amount to a kind of "sin squared," and make much more urgent my need to convince myself that the former *must* be nothing more than a once-in-a-lifetime aberration. So, while I'm somewhat relieved to know I can begin to unburden myself and talk with Father Tom now, I'm instantly unnerved. I've had no time to figure out how (or even if) I can muster the courage to speak the truth. On my short drive to the rectory, my mind flashes back and forth from laying out the whole truth to telling only some partial truth about what I've done. Yet in the back reaches of my mind, a distant voice reminds me that not telling the whole truth in Confession is itself considered a grievous sin—a bit of a Catch-22, I'm thinking.

It's my first time in the parish rectory, anywhere besides the church itself in fact. The office secretary points the way toward Father Tom's office, and I'm struck with the darkness of the hallway leading there along with the familiar, somewhat institutional, greenish tile walls, so similar to the foreboding look and feel of my St. Agatha grade school days. I spot Father Tom's nameplate and knock. As I enter, he gets up from behind his desk to say hello and shake hands. His smile is a welcoming one as he points to a chair just across his desk. There is no small talk. He asks right away, "So, what would you like to tell me about?" The phrasing of his question, not the more generic "what do you want to talk about," but the more personal friend-to-friend "what would you like to tell me about" actually serves to calm my nerves and slow down my accelerated heartbeat a bit. I immediately sense that he's not so much interested in hearing the facts of whatever I've done. He wants to listen to my story. He wants to know what's troubling me, what I'm feeling about whatever it is I've done.

Unrehearsed, I start slowly with a few background facts. I talk about my twelve years of Catholic schooling, say that I married young and have remained happily married for over thirty years, that we have two grown sons, and—to get into the heart of the matter—that I've never been unfaithful to my wife. Until now. I pause, but Father Tom simply looks me in the eyes intently and waits for me to go on. I explain that my work takes me away from home and all over the world, often for a few weeks at a time. At this point, I'm not conscious of my setting up plausible "grounds" for infidelity. But in hindsight, I suppose that I was subconsciously laying out some reasonably credibly rationale for why infidelity *might* happen now, but never in the previous years. Father Tom breaks his silence with a request, "Tell me the details."

Again, totally unrehearsed, I say what comes naturally to me—to the point that I'm not even sure what's coming next. I take him to faraway Kuala Lumpur, Malaysia. I say that in my tiredness and loneliness, I decided to do something I've always wondered about but had never engaged in: hire someone online for an in-room evening massage. Of course, working in Asia as long as I have, I've enjoyed a good many hotel spa massages and on-the-street foot massages—those of the more "professional" kind. In-room massages though, are not normally limited to professional muscle therapy. As to why I would, out of the blue, opt for one of these non-professional massages, I can only resort to the obvious: I wanted to feel good. So, as delicately as I can, I tell Father Tom that an attractive, young half Thai half Malay *woman* gently knocks on my door and proceeds to make me feel good. All the details Father Tom has requested are just so; except for that one minor detail about my massage visitor's gender.

No sooner have I slipped in this minor detail change that I hear a voice screaming inside my head: **What, in heaven's name, are you doing?** Honestly, to this day, I can truthfully say that I never pre-planned such a detail change. Call it "human instinct," or just plain self-esteem preservation naturally at work. Fortunately, despite the in-head screaming, Father Tom, perhaps to ease my nerves, simply says, "Okay, you sinned. You made a one-time mistake. But given the remote circumstances, there's no reason to assume it's anything more than that. Am I right?" To which I ever-so-softly reply, "Yes, that's right." So, we proceed on to complete the Sacrament of Confession. He asks that I say aloud an Act of Contrition. To my surprise, despite years and years since my last Confession, I somehow remember it nearly word-for-word. There's the absolution and a warm smile from Father Tom, and I'm free to go. We shake hands and just as I turn towards the office door, he makes one further request of me: "Before you go, tell me something you don't want me to know."

Never in my life have I heard such an unheard-of request. As I turn back to once again face Father Tom, nothing in the world could be clearer to me—I'm found out! I mean, in a lightning-bolt fashion, that there's no hiding the truth from the Man upstairs. Though momentarily paralyzed by Father Tom's stun-gun-like request, I'm certain that I smiled, maybe even shaking my head all the while. I realize that no matter how much you try to deny or disguise it, you just can't get away from telling the truth. If not now, then for sure, eventually. So, I sit myself down again in the chair across from him. Looking him in the eye, I see that he continues to smile warmly, approachable as ever. And here's the funny thing: whereas I might have expected a racing heartbeat and near hyperventilation after such an unexpected jolt of a request, I find that I'm more at ease than ever. Relieved, I'd say. Suddenly, I have an open invitation to come clean. To confess that I'm not just unfaithful, but I'm gay unfaithful. I give Father Tom this answer straightaway: "Everything I told you was true, except for one thing. The person giving me the massage was a young man, not a young woman."

"Oh, so you like boys," Father Tom replies—followed right after with, "And you lied." I nod my head, "Yes." But I want to say more. I tell him I cannot begin to understand how at fifty-plus, and married over thirty years, I can possibly be into guys; be gay. But I utter, "I must be" (still struggling to think or say outright that "I am"). Not so much that I haven't yet made up my mind. No, it's much more painful than that. I'm obviously not ready to accept the truth myself; not ready to *choose* to accept the truth **about** myself.

Which brings me back to the two deceptions I alluded to following my face-to-face admission to the man in the mirror: the self-deception that my first-ever sex with a gay guy meant nothing and wouldn't (couldn't be allowed to) happen again; and the "caught-in-the-act" confessional deception that my infidelity was of the more "forgivably normal" kind—with a sexy young woman. Where do such deceptions, denials, disbeliefs, whatever d-word you choose, come from? They come from *having to choose* to say who you are, to behave as you are, to **be** who you are, without the courage (yet) to do so. And so, the non-denying eyes, the relieved slumping shoulders, and the beginnings of that thin smile I perceived in my mirrored self-image represent a turning point for me. I can feel myself honestly—though slowly—coming out within.

STARTING TO THINK STRAIGHT—ABOUT COMING OUT

*"Normal is just a setting on
your washing machine."*

Besides good-naturedly granting me another shot at a legitimate (i.e., truthful) Confession, Father Tom does me one other big favor. He recommends a counselor whom I "might ought to talk with" to help me accept both who I am and how I am going to share this with the people I love the most. To the big questions of when and how I might eventually muster the courage to come out to my family and close friends, Father Tom calmly assures me, "You'll need some time, everyone in your place does; but be patient because I'm certain you'll *know* when. Once you're sure about yourself, that is. As to the how, well, I'd recommend you be as straightforward as you were with me—the second time, I mean." He laughs and then urges me to check back with him from time to time. He wants to know how things work out, for me, and for those to whom I come out.

I say that, in passing along the name and number of a potential counselor-listener, Father Tom did me a big favor. It was more than that. He opened a pathway that, by following it, would enable me to finally confront the choice I had been, up to then, running the opposite direction from. But I'm getting ahead of myself. Leaving my session with Father Tom, I'm still a few months away from my "Admit it. You're gay" mirror-admission. What transpires in those few months, with considerable help from my new-found counselor, gets me through coming out within, and on the verge of coming out without.

Let me get one thing off my chest straightaway: "coming out" is such a weak-dick term. Online searches show that its original usage denoted something quite different than it does today. In the early 1900s, it was a commonly used description borrowed from the ages-old, high-society practice of debutantes having their "coming out" balls or parties. Gays of the day apparently began using the same term, but to instead announce their joining with or "availability" within the gay subculture. What makes the term so weak today is the way it euphemistically disguises just how denuding and disrobing the act itself actually is.

Coming out isn't merely telling, admitting, or revealing; no. It's raw *exposing*. Imagine undressing naked in one of Macy's 5th Avenue windows. Only most gays I know would, in a heartbeat, prefer that kind of body-exposing to the opposing heart, mind, and soul-exposing they've gone through in coming out to families and friends. When one comes out, it isn't the same as stripping naked—it's worse. Those receiving the news almost always instantly call up images in their minds that are abhorrent, unimaginable, and disgusting even. Two males kissing, or worse yet, engaged in intercourse. For sure, coming out gay gives graphic meaning to "baring one's soul."

But here's the surprising thing about exposing: it always begets a *response*. And more often than not, the response we give ourselves is much less bearable than the one we get from others. We tend to think that what makes exposing our true, gay selves to others (especially to family) such a near impossible choice is our not being confident of an understanding and accepting response. Or conversely, being dead-certain of getting back nothing short of utter disappointment in us. But when we come out within, expose our gayness honestly—no, nakedly—to ourselves, the range and number of responses are far more devastating than feelings of disappointment. For example, before setting my first meeting with Father Tom's counselor, I find myself jotting down on scrap paper the internal voices, the automatic responses I can already hear if I truly believe and come to admit to myself that I'm gay:

What's wrong with me?
How could I be so shameful?
Who could possibly love me now, when I hate myself so?
If I'm not straight, am I no longer a real man?
I've always been 'normal'; now I'm not.

With self-responses like these, it is no wonder that coming out within so often gets disbelieved, denied, and delayed.

Such is my mindset as I sit for the first time in the counselor's waiting room. A typical professional's waiting room, though smaller and cozier than in most doctor's or dentist's offices. There are nondescript chairs along the wall, a few magazines neatly arranged on a side table, and not much in the way of wall art. Nor are there any other clients present. As I look around, all seems blandly familiar, except for a small printed sign hanging from the inside doorknob. It reads, "Normal is just a setting on your washing machine." I smile, even chuckle a bit upon seeing it. Hmmm . . . For someone definitely feeling not-normal, maybe this little sign portends a good beginning for me and my counselor, Joseph. At a minimum, some calming reassurance that I'm likely in the right place.

It isn't long before a hallway door opens quietly and an equally quiet, soft-spoken man of perhaps forty approaches me with hand extended: "Mike? Hi, I'm Joseph. Please, come along into my office." Following him into his office, my mind reverts automatically: I'm once again, as I was when about to first meet with Father Tom, unsure of what's about to happen, what I'm about to say. I don't mean that I'm once again contemplating (even unconsciously) some partial truth story. What would be the point? Been there, done that—with nothing but pitiful shame to show for it. No, rather, I'm simply feeling about as full of doubt as I can ever recall feeling, wondering "how can this guy help me answer those if-I'm-really-gay internal voices I keep hearing?" Lucky for me though, my doubt dissipates almost instantly. While I'm sitting myself down on Joseph's sofa, he smiles kindly and asks, "How do you think I might be able to help you?"

I should say that, when booking this first appointment with Joseph on the phone, it was little more than that. I merely mentioned that Father Tom from the university Catholic parish had suggested I contact Joseph, following a one-to-one conversation I had recently had at the parish rectory. So his question is a naïve, wide open one. And, much like Father Tom's initial "So what would you like to tell me about" question, this one from Joseph serves to gently open whatever door I wish to walk through. But there's something more in his opening words—not one, but two questions really. The obvious, "how might I be able to help you?"; but also the more subtle "how do *you think* I might be able to help you?" Of course, I didn't consciously separate these two parts at the time.

But, looking back, I'm certain that the more subtle one was the more self-confidence-building. Joseph isn't so much concerned with the typical service-supplier's "how can I help." He wants **me** to say what help I expect, I need, I hope for. Even at post midlife, I'm a novice when it comes to seeking any kind of personal counseling. Naturally, I've never done it before; hell, I've never needed it before. Or, if I'm plainly honest, I've never felt the (unmanly) weakness in seeking some kind of professional counseling. Why would I? I ought to be smart enough, strong enough to work things out for myself, right? So, being the novice that I am, I likely miss an essential counselor's principle: get the client focused on working through, coming to answers for himself.

Whatever Joseph's purpose, I find myself—doorknob sign fresh in my mind—making this reply: "I need help figuring out how the hell, so far along in my life, I became so fucking not-normal." As you might expect, Joseph asks me what I mean by "not normal" along with what sequence of events got me to feeling this way. I take him through much of the same story I shared with Father Tom: happily, longtime married with adult children; work having taken me all over the globe for years now; and, finally, the "catalytic" but self-revelatory moment with Vincent in far-off Malaysia. Joseph maintains sympathetic eye-contact all the while. He's listening closely, assuring me that he's interested. For all the emotional upheaval inside me, for all the shame and guilt I've been lugging around since Malaysia, and for assuming back then there would be no one I could possibly trust to "expose" myself to, I'm starting to feel more is in my favor than mere luck. The first two people I open up to—a Catholic priest and a psychotherapist, for God's sakes—might actually be able to help me get to where I'm going. Even if right now, I'm not at all sure I want to go there.

As I pause in my sequence of events story, Joseph softly

responds, "So, you're fifty-plus, having lived those fifty-plus years believing and behaving like you're straight. But now—after a first-ever, 'self-revealing' encounter with a young gay guy—you're fearing you might be gay, or, to use your words, not-normal. Shall we start with that?" For the remainder of our forty-five-minute session, we share our understandings of what "normal" means. No doubt sounding a bit defensive at first, I state that neither now, nor have I ever, regarded gays as being abnormal—especially in the Christian fundamentalist, stereotypical meaning of unnatural or deviant. I grew up with a gay cousin as my closest relative, after all. No, the "normal" I'm thinking about is more like "normal for me." And normal for me, from the time I can remember, has been: man, husband, father, and straight.

Joseph stops me to ask if I know the clinical definition of being gay (as it applies in its more common use to males). I don't. He makes it real simple: "Being gay means you **only** want to have sex with men." His point, he says, in bringing this up is that, putting whether you're normal or not aside, you can't think of yourself as, call yourself, or actually *be* gay unless it's true that you only want to have sex with other men. The obvious next question he asks, then: "Does this describe you, now?" But he doesn't wait for me to answer. Instead he goes on, "That's probably an unfair question for our first time together. We can put it on hold for a bit. And, if you're comfortable as we keep talking, I'd like to hear more about your sense of and sensations about your own sexual attractions. I mean, you've been married a long while, in a heterosexual relationship, but you've only very recently experienced your first homosexual relationship. We ought to work through your feelings about both in some detail. By the way, if it helps make you more comfortable sharing these feelings, I also happen to be gay."

Given his soft-spoken manner and perhaps a hint of his body language during our first moments together, I suppose I wondered if Joseph might not be simply a counselor, but a gay counselor to boot. But hearing him so nonchalantly coming out to me, I **do** feel comfortable. Even better, I feel relieved. My mind flashes back to that first choice I made to unload that inundating post-Vincent burden of guilt, to start grappling with who the hell I really was. What appeared to be, upon first consideration, a near-impossible choice—to seek out a priest and confess my sins—now, with the subsequent introduction to Joseph, looks to have been a choice with some hopeful possibility. So, I tell Joseph that I agree; we do need to examine my sexual attraction history. What signals, throughout that history, have I received? More critically, what *feelings*, what indicators have I either consciously or unconsciously chosen to overlook . . . just say it, deny?

Our time together in this first meeting blazes by. Joseph suggests I think about these feelings, even jot down some observations and bring them along next time, if it helps. Before our time runs out, he wants to revisit my feelings of not-normalcy. He admits to understanding how, after fifty-plus years of self-perception as a straight guy, I could now feel self-betrayed. But he wants to offer me another perspective on normalcy. He puts it this way: "Normal isn't about *who* someone is, it's about pursuing *what needs* that someone is missing. Take that crucial, lifetime happiness need of finding and enjoying an enduring, loving intimacy with another person: if that need isn't being met, what's 'normal' is to relentlessly seek out a way to meet it."

As to when a person might actually meet that need, who can say? Different times for different guys. To add a bit of substance, though, Joseph cites what he calls the *S-O Continuum*—the sexual-orientation progression or sequence that runs, say, from far right (that would be straight) to far left (gay or lesbian), with other orientation "stops" along the line. He hastens to add, smiling, that there's no stop labeled "normal" on the continuum. As Joseph goes on to explain, while it's commonly thought that one's sexual orientation is self-evident at or around puberty, in reality there is no set, flip-the-switch time. In fact, many individuals start out at neither end of the continuum and, over a period of years, move one way or another. Gravitate, so to speak, to their natural SO.

Hearing Joseph's take on the meaning of normal, along with his layman's look at the SO Continuum, has the intended effect: I already feel less alone, less not-normal than when we first shook hands forty-five minutes ago. You could say that he's been priming me, to get my thinking straight about coming out. Normally, we would agree to meet again in a week; but I have an extended international business trip booked for the next few. So, we set our next session for more than three weeks away. As he walks me to the door (where I once again spy the real definition of normal hanging there), he asks where my upcoming travels will take me. I tell him first, "Asia." But then, my mind imagining things to come, I add, "With most of my time in Bangkok."

THE THAI ATTRACTION
"Don't think too much."

I entered Thailand for the first time in my life on a business trip around 1990. That was long before I had any fantasies about connecting with an online male escort. That would also be long before any need for confessions and counseling. No, I arrived in Thailand that very first time imagining myself securely set as a normal, All-American, straight guy. But, answer me this: why is it that on that very first visit, I find myself taxi-bound and Bangkok gridlock-traffic bound, staring through the back seat windows, as if star-struck, at so many handsome—no, a better word is beautiful—young Thai guys passing us left and right on the sidewalks? Slim, trim bodies, square-chiseled faces, silky jet-black hair. I'm not hypnotized; more like magnetized. Where in the world does such an alluring, same-sex auto-attraction—in a normal, All-American straight guy—come from?

Funny, I recall little else about that initial trip. I've already alluded, though, to a building and then on-going seemingly innate attraction to younger Asian men, none stronger than towards Thai's. It's only natural, then, looking ahead to my upcoming trip to Bangkok (preceded by others to Asia and Thailand in between), that I'm once again daydreaming about the sexy Thai "eye candies" I'm assured of enjoying while there. But—intermingled with flashes of my telling moment with Vincent in Kuala Lumpur—I'm already thinking eye candy alone mightn't be nearly enough.

Fast-forward a bit and I've arrived in Bangkok a few days before my client work is set to start. I'm staying at a classically Thai five-star hotel (with colorfully stunning, two-story high, floor-to-ceiling lobby murals depicting scenes from historic Thai and Buddhist legends) that's a stone's throw from the Ratchadamri Skytrain Station. That means I'm within one sky-train stop of Saladaeng Station, centered in the hub of the hustling, ever-touristy, and go-go bar dense district known as Silom. Though I'm familiar with the district's (especially, its nucleus, Patpong's) legendary sex trade reputation, I've never been anywhere near it. Hell, up to now, on those few previous trips to Bangkok, I've barely left the hotels I was eating, sleeping, and working in. I'm not really attracted to the sounds of Patpong hawkers, even less to the sights of the go-go girl pole dance and ping-pong ball shows they tout. But with the few days I have free this time, there's one attraction in Silom that I find far more appealing, or should I say, *tempting*? Tucked away here and there, typically on small side alleyways Thai's call *sois*, are discreetly named clubs—some operating out of small-to-medium sized houses—that offer "massage for men."

Sooner than I think, I will learn in more detail how these club-houses work. You enter and are immediately welcomed by an attractive front desk boy-host (who, by the way, is like everyone else working there, "available" should you desire his services). He politely ushers you to a cushiony sofa arranged for viewing a kind of staging area, with mirrors, benches, and barbells surrounding the staging perimeter. He asks if you would like to order a beer or cocktail, all the while a steady line of athletically slim-to-muscled, bikini-clad, young adult guys take up places in front of you—and smile. Your host invites you to look over all the boys and let him know which one you choose. Of course, with an instant influx of as many as thirty to forty handsome guys smiling at you, making a snap choice can be difficult. No matter, the host can recommend someone, if you like. He can also answer any and all—even sexually specific—questions you may have about any of the boys. What he won't tell you, though (unless you know enough to ask), is that about half the boys are gay and half are straight. Nor will he tell you which is which.

But before I'm introduced to all this, and no less than a few weeks after my "can never happen again" encounter in gay-unfriendly Malaysia, I find myself sensually scrolling through Silom's concentrated massage-for-men websites. I'll later in life come to fondly regard Silom as the "center of the gay universe." Though I didn't mention it in my retelling of that first-time with Vincent in Kuala Lumpur, getting to the point of hiring and booking him wasn't without some trepidation. First-time gay sex jitters, sure. But much more than that were the internal nerve-racking forces competing for the behavior I would choose. On one side, *"You can't do this. After thirty-plus years of faithful marriage and the respectful pride of two grown sons, you simply cannot 'try out' gay sex—with someone more than thirty years younger than you. Younger, even, than your two sons! You would never be able to live with yourself."* On the other side, *"You're over fifty, damn it. And you know you've been thinking about this for a long time now. This isn't about 'trying out' something; it's about finding out something. If you don't start finding out now, when will you? When you're way too old for it to matter anymore, or worse yet, for any guy in the world to even look at you, let alone care—like at sixty or seventy?"*

I recall this trepidation, these fighting factions in my head and heart now. As I once again taste the urge, the desire to meet up with another young, gay Thai, my fears and self-doubts are further amplified. How could they not be? I put myself through the hell of a bad confession and at the forgiving mercy of a (thankfully kind) Catholic priest. All with the hopeful intent of going forth and sinning gay no more. And while it's true I took my leave of Father Tom asking him when and how I might ultimately come out to myself and to my family, I neither left his office nor first entered Joseph's at all convinced that I was once straight but now am gay. So right now, as I can easily and very privately walk to that center of the gay universe, the "other side" voice in my head is, once again, the louder one: Am I gay? I **do** need to keep finding out—but it's impossible to do so solo. As Joseph so recently instructed me, "being gay means you only want to have sex with men."

This time, his name is Joe. Well, his English nickname, that is. I won't learn his Thai name until later. I have left the dubious sanctity of my hotel with a guide map in hand. Among the several boy-massage houses scattered around the Silom area, there is one which appears on the map to be easier to find. That's because it's not located on one of those many, typically unmarked, side alleyway sois.Rather, it looks to be within a three-story open-courtyard set of connected shops approximately a mile up from the hotel, along the four-lanes of Silom Road. This is to be my destination, a second-story club in the Silom Plaza named HIS. It's not an abbreviation, simply the English pronoun for the male gender. After a longer-than-expected and much sweatier-than-expected walk (it is hot season in Thailand), I stagger into the cooler shadows of Silom Plaza courtyard. I look up and around me, and see, not a HIS logo sign, but four or five bikini-clad boys deliciously leaning and waving over the second floor balcony railing. I believe I've arrived.

Vincent was good-looking. Shy, but innocently cool. Joe is . . . stunning. Drop-dead handsome and, on first impressions alone, anything but shy—more like innately charismatic. Posing and smiling, he stands among twenty-five or more amazing looking guys, all eyes on me, the customer. But I only see him. Or, should I say, his smile. How can it be that, with a taut, slim body and chiseled square, smooth-skinned and lightly tanned face, that it's the smile alone that says, "Choose me. I'm sexy"? But that's what it is, what makes the boy-host, who has been not-so-sneakily watching my eyes move and then lock on, turn to me, and ask, "Oh, I see Joe's the one you want?"

My host signals for Joe to come join us. As he approaches, Joe *sawadee's* me, in the typical Thai way of greeting someone by making prayer hands and bringing them up to the face while saying, *"Sawadee, krup."* Though I speak no Thai, like most tourists I have learned this polite way to say hello or good day when meeting or greeting someone in Thailand. Up close, Joe's charismatic smile brightens as if on high beam. I know I'm staring, but such a smile—running from full thick lips to cavern-deep brown eyes—has a hypnotic effect. He asks my name and repeats it back to me. He tells me his name is Joe, and points the way for me to follow him to a one of the private HIS massage rooms. Neither of us speaks as we enter the dimly lit aroma-scented room. Lemongrass,

I assume. He nods toward the corner shower, still smiling innocently, but eagerly. As I catch my reflection in the glass shower door, I'm struck by the breadth on my own smile. Must be contagious.

I've agreed with the host to pay for a one-hour oil massage. As to the massage itself though, I recall very little. I suppose this is because, while the physical part of it was wonderfully satisfying, it was much like the pleasure I had experienced with Vincent. The one thing about this first time alone with Joe that I definitely **do** recall is that selfsame, seemingly drug-induced sensation of being totally at ease in my own skin. Of being my naturally normal self. Only this time, that exhilarating sensation doesn't morph quite so easily into dreaded shame and its ensuing guilt.

Perhaps this repeating pattern, first with Vincent then with Joe, of paying a young, gay guy for incidental sex would seem to mean that I'm merely living out my counselor, Joseph's, basic definition of being gay. Of the intensity of my sexual attraction to young, cool, Asian guys, there can be no doubt. And this attraction, of course, is central to my evolving sense of "naturally normal self." But soon after meeting Joe, I discover that there is an equally intense, alternate attraction that's also key to being (no, becoming) my "naturally normal self." Though I'm not consciously aware of it at the moment, what I will soon find I hunger for much more than oneoff gay sex encounters involves developing an intimate relationship; with a younger gay guy, naturally. The thing is, I already know I can find (okay, pay) a young, cool, gay Thai guy for sex—that's easy. But could I possibly ever find a young, cool, gay Thai boyfriend?

It's hard to say exactly when and where this impossible dream of mine began—to one day, meet and fall for a younger Thai guy, and, the impossible part, have him fall for me. It could be that the beginnings happened here, meeting Joe (who, though I'm unaware of it then, will in time become much more to me than a close friend). But not so much from the physical contact of the massage itself as from the getting-to-know-you contact right afterwards. Showering and then getting dressed, we start up the first of many future conversations. The usual kind of thing to start. Though Joe's English vocabulary is limited and his grammar street-learned, he understands and speaks a good deal better English than my minimalist hello, excuse me, and thank you Thai. He asks me where I'm from and a question right after which I will discover is a common one coming from massage and bar boys throughout gay Bangkok: "How long will you stay in Thailand?" It's not merely a polite, normal kind of thing to ask a tourist; the inquiry provides a discreet estimate of how many more times one might be available as a customer. I tell him I'll be in Bangkok for work nearly the entire week, though after tomorrow I'll be busy with my clients most of the time. For some reason, though, I also add, "I might have a few nights free." Again, he flashes that amazing, alluring smile!

Dressed and collected, we find a small table in the HIS lobby area, opposite a small but Johnnie Walker Red and Chivas Regal stocked bar that I had barely noticed when I first arrived. I ask what Joe would like to drink, which turns out to be the same for me. He orders two Singha beers—over ice. I return his initial question to me: "Where are *you* from? Bangkok, or some other place in Thailand?" He replies, "I am from Esan . . . Thai country . . . a small village named Bua Yai." As I'm not familiar with Esan, nor with very much else about Thailand's geography or culture, I ask him to tell me more about Esan: What part of Thailand? How is it different from the rest of Thailand? What do most people do there? Quite proudly, Joe informs me that Esan is a large portion of northeast Thailand, comprising the original lands forming today's country boundaries. In fact, he says, Thailand has two official languages: Esan and Thai, which use the same alphabet but sound quite different when spoken. Very few Bangkok or southern-born Thai's can speak Esan. I'm getting the picture a bit—something like Catalan and Spanish in Spain, I assume. Lastly, he adds that most people living in Esan are farmers, like his big family.

I want to ask him more about his family. But before I have the chance, he mentions one further distinction between the two main cultures within Thailand, Esan Thai and Chinese Thai. Unsure of what he's trying to say, but being all ears, I'm listening to learn. He begins by telling me how much he would like to have "bright, white" skin like me. His skin—like most sunbaked farmer-types from Esan—is dark (though to me, I'd call his skin more favorably tanned, akin to the color of skin most Westerners avidly seek from beaches and tanning booths). As we struggle a bit through our translated back-and-forth's and limited vocabularies, I eventually get his meaning. Esan people, both women and men, perceive pure, white skin as the beauty standard. Laughing, I somehow get him to understand that it's funny we Westerners think the opposite. We think light-brown, tanned skin—like his—is the most to be desired. Grinning, he nods that he understands, and he tells me that most Chinese Thai's already have much lighter skin than Esan Thai's, and because of that they also tend to look down on Esan Thai's, who are "dark-skinned," "farmers," and "country."

I've already alluded, upon first sight, to Joe's stunning, drop-dead good looks. So, I can't contain myself, complimenting him on his striking handsomeness as we clank glasses and down our Singha's. I tell him that his squared facial features are considered classic by most Westerners, especially his high cheekbones. Not having any idea how to communicate "cheekbones" in even simpler English, I reach across and lightly trace my finger around those prominent bones just under his eyes. He gets it and laughs, yet again self-deprecatingly saying something in reply like, "Oh no! This part of my face is too big, stands out too much." He adds that his non-Esan Thai friends at HIS routinely poke fun at his bony Esan cheeks, insisting he has *puukao* (in English, mountains) not-normal cheeks on his face. I return the laugh but insist equally that, to me, his mountains make his face look super-sexy.

Delighting so much in our easy chatting, along with the buzz from sharing another couple of beers, I lose track of the time. I notice that HIS gets busier. More customers are now sitting in front of the boy staging area. I don't want our first time together to end, but I'm aware that, as stand-out handsome as he is, Joe might easily pick up another customer today. So, I tell him I need to go back to my hotel, do some prep-work for my clients. But I need to tip him, though I have no idea what tip amount is usual, what he expects. As I move toward the counter, Joe follows closely alongside me. The boy host confirms the one-hour oil massage price of 1500 baht (about fifty dollars), which I pay in Thai baht. With Joe standing close by, however, it's too awkward to ask the host what tip is right (I will learn before my next visit, though, that massage boys typically expect and get one to two-thousand-baht tips). I'm carrying some large U.S. dollar denominations, which is what I used to pay Vincent in Malaysia. So, without even thinking, I discreetly slip Joe a $100 Ben Franklin. His face tells me instantly that I've exceeded the mark. Thanking me in Thai—with several *Krup khun, krups*—he lightly holds my upper arm and guides me out the entrance door, then down a few steps away from other HIS boys outside on the courtyard balcony.

Joe wants to know if I will come back to see him at

HIS again. Naturally, he's still grinning broadly and I'm getting the impression he kind of likes me. Well, let's say he definitely likes Ben Franklin! I **do** want to see him again. I ask him what time he gets off work today, and he tells me 10 p.m. But, he hastens to add, if I'd like to pay the front desk 500 baht, he can leave work early and meet me at my hotel later. Now *I'm* grinning. I hand him a 500 baht note and ask if he's familiar with my hotel. He knows it well, and no wonder because, as I will also soon learn, Bangkok massage boys earn more of their daily income outside of HIS than inside—callouts are a big deal. So, we'll meet up in the hotel lobby at eight. On the walk back to the hotel, I stop at an Asia Books store to purchase a decent Thai-English dictionary. Until we each get bigger vocabularies, and since I definitely want us to keep talking, passing the little book back and forth can serve us as a silent interpreter.

At our agreed-to time, I spot Joe in the hotel lobby as I step out from the lift. Though always a bit crowded, finding his oversized smile among the many lobby guests is easy. I ask if he has eaten, if he's hungry, and if so, does he know someplace good we can walk to. Turns out, he has a favorite seafood place located within a ten-minute walk. It sits alongside the super-popular Lumpini Night Bazaar, where every night, tourists from everywhere can shop until after midnight and buy copy-everything. Over more beers (this time, Leo; a less heavy, less expensive, but Esan-preferred brand brewed also by Singha) and seven or eight extra-spicy-hot dishes I let Joe order, we talk some more. With my tongue on fire, I realize at once why Thai's insist upon drinking their beer over ice. In between cooling gulps, I ask Joe to tell me about his family in Esan.

Joe relates that he is the youngest of nine children. His parents—farmers from Bua Yai—both died when he was quite young. His much older sister, Hong, pretty much raised him as a surrogate mom. As for schooling, while he started elementary school at the local Buddhist temple school like other boys in his district, around age ten his older brothers sent him to a *muy thai* school, where he mainly trained to become a competitive Thai kickboxer. (In the future, I will not only accompany Joe to some *muy thai* boxing matches at the world-famous Lumpini Muy Thai Arena, but he will also proudly tell me that, as a teenager, he competed at Lumpini—in fact, was once a champion there in his age-weight division.) Again, despite the ever-handy Thai-English dictionary on the table, our limited casual conversation skills in each other's native language means—in between eating and drinking—we need a lot of book passing to really understand one another. During a lull, Joe asks me, what about *my* family? I say, "Let's drink up, get the check, and head back to my hotel room. We can relax and I'll tell you my story there."

Maybe it's the number of beers, or more likely pure libido at work. Having been staring as if spellbound for a few hours now at one of the sexiest guys I've ever seen, once inside my room, I'm in the mood for some intimacy. No massage is needed this time. Joe, undoubtedly expecting something like this, couldn't be more at ease, more obliging. Removing his T-shirt, I'm struck anew: he still *does* have the tightly muscled body of a *muy thai* guy. I find our time together on the bed more intoxicating than all the alcohol we've consumed: truly, I cannot recall a single moment in my life when pleasure has felt this good.

Afterwards, showered and over some whiskey and Coke from the mini-bar, we sit closely side-by-side on the room's love seat, wearing the hotel's terrycloth robes. We talk some more. I tell Joe that I'm married, have been married a long time in fact, and have two grown sons. When he understands that I mean adult sons, I can see some surprise on his face. Before he can ask, I admit to being older than I probably look, in my early fifties. For some reason I still can't explain, the admission of my age sends a slap my way. As if waking up and suddenly realizing what I thought was a fantasy dream, is actually a nightmare of sorts. It's that taint of guilt rearing itself up again, and I hear: *"I'm fifty-something, for God's sake. I've been married for almost thirty years. What the fuck am I doing?"* Joe detects the change in my happy mood. In the pause of the silence, he asks me guardedly, "Your family knows you are gay?"

I shake my head; no. I take a few breaths and then reply, "No one knows. I'm not sure I know. But I must be gay . . . and I cannot stop worrying about how I might ever tell my wife, my sons." For a young guy I just met and who, like me, is struggling to understand nearly everything each of us is saying, I nevertheless discern some genuine sympathy in Joe's eyes. I haven't asked his age, but I'm guessing he's all of twenty-one or two. But what he says next sounds a lot older and wiser. He says he can tell, even in the few hours we've known each other, that I'm a very kind guy; he calls me *jai di* in Thai, which means kind-hearted, and happens to be one of the nicest compliments any Thai can pay to a foreigner. He says to relax, to be patient and wait, like the Buddha. And not be so serious about things. But it's what he says next that best soothes the sting of that slap I felt: "Don't think too much." I crack a smile. Now that's something to think about.

INTERPRETING THE THAI ATTRACTION

"Hello, honey. Welcome."

I **do** keep thinking about Joe's advice; thinking, paradoxically, about "not thinking too much." But more specifically, besides his intent to ease my mind and lift my spirits some, what was Joe getting at, *really*? At first, I suppose I took his words to mean something like, "hey, you're in Thailand, having more than a few feel-good drinks, and enjoying being here with me. So, enjoy it!" Though clearly not occurring to me at the time, Joe was instinctively extending me a fairly typical Buddhist-Thai kind of precept: be present, live in the moment. Only later, after Joe returned to his Bangkok apartment sometime around 2 a.m., still not sleepy and having sobered up a bit more, did I think further—or maybe better said—did I take to heart other implications from Joe's advice to me, regardless of whether he ever intended them.

Sparring within my conscience are conflicting thoughts,

starting with: *"Of course, I'm thinking a lot—too much even. Hell, I'm having THE identity crisis of my life, unsure of, after five decades of relative certainty, who I really am. What else could I expect? And, how can I not think about the impending disaster and doom I'm going to rain down upon the three people I love the most in the world; once I totally, fully, absolutely accept I'm gay—not straight?"* Rebutted instantly by, *"Still, Joe's words carry an implied, important truth: we Western-minded (and Christian-trained) types do tend to overthink everything, to find ways for making ourselves miserably guilty over almost anything."*

Incapable at this crazy hour of resolving either side of this mental conflict, I find that one conclusion of sorts, somehow, does begin to form. I ask myself: What's the single most hopeful thing I've learned so far, from talking honestly—sharing my thinking—with Father Tom, with Joseph, and though so very briefly, with Joe? It's this: finding someone I can trustfully talk to, to sort my thinking out with, helps me immensely. Even more so when that someone is gay. Lying down, closing my eyes, I start calculating ways to spend as much time with Joe as I can before I must head home. I've got a feeling, even minus a common language, Joe's going to be, at the very least, a much-needed, kindhearted (as in jai di) listener. More than this, as I drift off (or maybe I'm already dreaming) I wonder: Have I've found my first gay friend?

Joe had asked me, after my first visit to HIS, if I would come there to see him again. Upon awakening, as if picking right up where my slumberous mind left off, I'm instantly imagining, eagerly anticipating another afternoon visit to HIS. In fact, as Joe was leaving last night, we spoke about meeting up at HIS again today, even exchanged mobile numbers. These being the very early days of texting, it's most common to communicate by voice, though even this has its limitations since my number is an international one (requiring a caller to have an international dialing plan on his cell). Joe's number is +66 Thai-only. I can call him, but he cannot call me. So, we agreed I would arrive at HIS around 3 p.m. The massage clubs open as early as 1 p.m., but since customers rarely make their way to them until the cocktail hours, most of the high-demand boys don't arrive until 3 or later. It's a perfect confluence of attractive young guys and alcohol. After all, these clubs make their money from both boys and beer.

As it's only running on noon, I still have some time before embarking upon my second walk to HIS, along sure-to-be sweltering Silom Road. Time to turn certain things over in my head: *"I'm attracted to Joe—why? Sexually attracted, duh! But there's something else. I felt it last night as we sat close together and talked. He seems to really want to get to know me, and I don't think it's merely because I'm a high-paying customer. He actually likes to listen. And I don't think you can easily fake that."* Besides the sex, there's no doubt I'm rejuvenated by his youthful exuberance. By his larger-than-life, straight-from-the-heart smile. It's suddenly easy to forget how old I am in the company of someone who expresses himself so naturally, so innocently. Which prompts again that question that was last on my mind last night: might Joe be my very first, potentially close, gay friend? The question no sooner recurs, than a corollary question (from where?) follows: *"Joe is gay, isn't he?"* But I dismiss the question about as quickly as it occurs. Of course Joe's gay. He works at a gay massage club; he stays with gay guys in their hotels; he has sex with gays all the time. Must be.

Returning to HIS, I'm welcomed by my beaming front-desk host as if I've been a regular for some time. Clearly, Joe has spread the word. But no need this time to position me in front of the staging area, nor for the usual parade of bikini-boys. The host will fetch Joe from the back room. Meanwhile, he politely suggests I sit at the corner bar, maybe start with a cold Leo. With a *sawadee* and a full-tooth smile, Joe once again greets me. He asks what I've been up to. I tell him, "Not much . . . just killing time until I can see you again." He flashes an aw-shucks kind of smile, but I know he appreciates the compliment. As I've not yet ordered a drink, he wonders if I'd like something cold, or instead, something hot—like another oil massage first. Grinning I say, "let's do oil first, beer second." The massage is, yet again, super-satisfying, heavenly even. Especially the parts that are not technically a massage.

Having showered together and now seated once again across each other in the HIS bar area, I ask if he is free—I mean, if it's okay to pay the club again for him to leave with me. It is. It always is, assuming, of course, the boy wants to go. Joe does. While he changes into street clothes, I sip a cold one. And I'm suddenly famished. It is getting on to dinner time, anyhow. Looking coquettishly sexy fully clothed, Joe says he, too, is quite hungry and suggests we eat down below HIS, on the courtyard level. There's a family-run Chinese restaurant he frequents there, where the roast duck is especially *aroi* (that's, tasty). Before we head down, he asks if I mind inviting a few HIS friends to join us. It's fine with me, which is just as well since asking friends to join will—I'll soon discover—become the norm. Within five minutes or so, three young, handsome HIS guys (though none as Esan-striking as Joe) join us, each offering to shake my hand, Western style. I meet yet another guy named Joe, Tak, and Man. Each is eagerly friendly, though none has much in the way of English at hand. No matter. Joe is elated to have them join us. And if Joe's happy, I'm very happy!

With the sun well gone, and some gentle cooling breezes, we pull up a table outside the restaurant in the middle of the courtyard. Over the roast duck and a good many other assorted dishes, mostly unrecognizable to me, there is much Thai chatter. Every so often, Joe stops to ask, "Mike, you OK?" And, sometimes, to explain a little of what the guys are talking about. It's a strange feeling, hearing so much but listening so little. Which I'll find, much as inviting Thai friends to join us, is going to be the way of many days and nights in my Thai future. But even being pretty much left out, I'm pleased to see that Joe and his friends are enjoying themselves. Sure, enjoying a free meal, but amongst all the joking and laughter (and considerable beer drinking) definitely enjoying their time together. With eating and drinking winding down—and the other HIS guys needing to get back to work during customer primetime—Joe asks me if I'd like him to go back to the hotel with me. I would, but I know I've got a very early morning get-up plus a full day's work with client's approaching. So, reluctantly, I tell him I'd better go back alone. But, I assure Joe I'll see him again as soon as I can. I ask what days he's working this week, adding that I can always call him to make sure he's available. He hugs me warmly as I leave, says he will be waiting for me, and laughing, reminds me, "Don't think too much."

Ironically, I find I cannot stop thinking too much—about Joe, that is, and how incredibly attracted to him I'm becoming. Much as I hate the wait to be with him again, client work absorbs all daytime and would-be free night-times over the next few days. I am not able to meet up with Joe—until my last evening in Bangkok, a Friday. In addition to yet another Ben Franklin I slipped Joe as I left a few nights ago, I handed him enough Thai baht to pay for his "release" from the club, so as to be free to meet up with me come Friday. And, as it's my last night in Bangkok this trip, I greedily want as much time with him as I can get.

Friday arrives. Having finished all my client work for the week around 3 p.m., I hurry to call Joe. We've talked by phone almost every day since last seeing each other, but our language shortcomings become amplified when we're not face-to-face. I've felt so constrained in expressing myself, and now at last I'm free—and eager. Joe says he wants to make this last night in Bangkok fun for me, and he has a couple of places he would like to take me. First, he wonders, do I play snooker? Never, I tell him, though I admit to having played some eight-ball pool as a kid, and not at all well. But I'm open to trying snooker, so we agree to meet at the corner of Silom and Soi Pi Phat, about two-thirds of the way from the hotel to HIS. There's a snooker parlor on Pi Phat Joe knows and likes because, he says, he knows the manager there. The snooker girls (who rack the games and serve you drinks) are sexy, and we can drink Singha while playing.

I spy Joe standing near the corner from a block and a half away, his smile broadening as he also spots me walking his way. We *sawadee* each other and he leads me down Soi Pi Phat, passing, along the route, a boutique kind of hotel called Silom Serene. Joe points it out and suggests I stay here next time: it's nice but not too expensive, a five to ten-minute walk from HIS, and (as with the snooker parlor we're headed to) he knows the hotel manager. He says she is very jai di. In my mind pops an automatic observation: Joe must know lots of hotel/entertainment people and places around here—around Silom, the center of the gay and go-go girl universe. But then again, he ought to, given his line of work. What I'll find is more telling about him, after being with him several more times in the months ahead, though, is the sharpness—more like cleverness, really—of his street smarts. For what I don't know now but will later learn is that, in his brief twenty-two years, Joe has gone from *Muay Thai* champion, to street-cart fruit seller, to office delivery boy, to taxi driver, to as of now, massage boy. And what savvy survival skills he has already mastered have come not so much from the school as from the streets.

The snooker parlor resides up some rickety outdoor stairs of a nondescript building I otherwise would have failed to notice. Once inside, Joe's manager-friend greets us most sociably and shows us to an open table. I've seen snooker matches, rarely, on Thai TV but had never appreciated just how large the snooker tables are, nor how long the snooker cue sticks are. I'm already laughing out loud, imagining how poorly I'm bound to perform with these Olympic-sized versions of pool. Thankfully, even before one of the cute, young snooker girls racks us up, beer and ice are set upon a side table. I believe Joe called this right: we're not here so much to play snooker, but to down icy cold *bia Singh*. Even better, our petite, sexy snooker-server girl is right by to pour for us, though her eyes are mainly upon Joe. Why not? It's easy to see how his sexy good looks and magnetic personality entice both gays and gals.

Snooker turns out to be a load of laughs, thanks largely

to so many off-the-mark shots mostly by me, but some also by Joe. Each becomes cause for another clink of beer mugs. We end up playing and drinking for a couple of hours. As it's nearing 9 p.m., Joe asks for our check. He has another destination for us, where things get going between nine and ten. Joe recommends the right tip for his sexy-server friend (though I never understood a thing they said during our games, I had no trouble noticing their connection). As we descend to Soi Pi Phat, Joe informs me we'll walk from Silom to a nearby, parallel main road, Surawong. There's a popular soi running off Surawong Joe wants me to see, with lots of bars, outdoor seating, flashing neon, and, I'm guessing, some weekend action.

Although he neglected to mention it during our walk over, the most noteworthy feature of our destination flashes out in every neon bar sign overhanging the soi: Dream Boys, X Boys, Fresh Boys, Future Boys, and Boys of Bangkok. It's a mini-version of old-town Las Vegas, only rainbow style. As we enter from Surawong, slim, barely legal waiter-boys in short-shorts and tank-tops holding drink menus reach out to lightly tug my arm, smiling and saying "Hello, honey. Welcome." Others merely ogle Joe as we push our way forward. I get it, we've hit the epicenter of Bangkok's gay universe. With my head tacking left then right, it is all I can do to keep Joe—a few steps ahead—in sight. Luckily, before I am shanghaied by one of many the doormen touts lining the soi, Joe grasps my hand and draws me into the bar he has in mind, Boys of Bangkok.

The bar is filling up fast, but there are still choice seats available. No sooner do we step inside that a probably late-twenties looking, black sport-coat wearing guy flashes his laser light towards our seats. I notice there's a plastic number pin attached to his lapel, #99. Inside, it's loud with bar-beat blaring overhead, so Joe leans in close and tells me this guy is a captain. Every bar in the soi has perhaps three to four captains who act as kind of maître d's and supervise a harem of charming waiter-boys. Our captain has led us to one of the many faux leather black booths that surround and face in a U-type layout a strobe-lighted stage, which stands about two feet above floor level. Our butts barely touch the booth-seat when the captain puts a drink-price list in front of us, asking what we would like. The choices are pretty much beer, whiskey and soda (Johnnie Walker Red or Black), or Bacardi Breezer. Each runs 250 baht (about eight dollars). We opt for the easily familiar Singha. While waiting for the drinks, I peruse the crowd: mainly foreigners (*farang* in Thai) like me; some obviously gay couples; about half solo farang accompanied by a Thai. And of that half, in nearly every instance, the foreigner is older and the Thai is younger. Mirror images of us.

We clink our bottles together in a toast. I've learned fast: with Thai's, one beer bottle will likely endure several toasts, always expressed with the Thai version of good luck, *Chook dii*. Joe checks my face for a smile and asks once again what will become a common question of me, "Mike, you okay, right?" I smile readily, grab his upper arm, and squeeze it. Sure! With some momentary lull in the DJ's thump-thump decibel level, Joe says that he doesn't come here often, but that they have a boy show that is super-popular, especially with tourists (that would be, gay tourists, naturally). The show will start shortly. For now, the stage is nearly jammed with what must be fifty slim, eighteen-to-twenty something guys, each wearing the same Boys of Bangkok embossed bikini with their mobile phones sticking out and above the ass side of their briefs. Every thirty seconds or so, the boys rotate to their right, circling around the stage in such a way that no matter where a customer is seated, he can eventually have a good look at any boy. Oh, and as with the captains and waiters, each boy also has a red plastic number pinned to his bikini, making it as convenient as possible for a customer to "call someone over" for a drink, a chat, and to see what develops.

The show. To say I could never have imagined what I was about to watch would be a gross understatement. Not merely because I'm in a gay bar for the first time in my life. The first few acts are tame enough: a candle show, a shower show, soft porn stuff. That much I might expect. No, it's what happens in the last act, the "main event" so to speak, that dumbfounds me. For the finale—what, I realize later, most all of the foreign customers have really come to see—in the dim pre-act lighting, two waiters jump to the stage and pull down some not so cleverly concealed monkey bars and gymnastic rings in the center. Then with some lightly romantic Kenny G-like instrumental wafting from overhead, two very attractive, nearly naked boys enter the stage, one wearing an open-front robe, the other only a G-string. Their "clothes" give them away: robe is Top, G-string is Bottom. Following some slow massage, strobe lights kick in. The music volume and tempo accelerate, KY and condoms appear, and well, the couple connects—in full view of everyone. No need to describe how they proceed to take swinging advantage of the gymnastic props. Somewhere in the middle of this, Joe looks at me with a huge grin. He asks, "Did you see show like this before? You have something like this in U.S.?" As I'm literally stage-struck, all I can do is shake my head. No—never.

With the show over, the many boys working in the bar are fast up on stage doing their rotations. Even though the majority of customers leave right after the finale, some linger—like us—to drink a bit, talk and smoke. Joe says this is his first time to see such a sex show with two guys doing it; I'm thinking, maybe or maybe not. But it's okay with me, because we've had a fun time tonight, at snooker and here in the soi, just as he promised. It's pushing 12:30 a.m. and the bar closes at 1. So, we take our time leaving and walking toward Surawong. Joe asks if I'd like him to go back to the hotel with me. I would, in the worst way. But I know I've got an airport car around 5 a.m. and I tell him, sighing, "Let's wait until next time." He right away asks when that might be. I tell him I have no firm date, but I will definitely be back—to see him. Loitering at the soi's entrance, with me not wanting our time together to end, I suggest we exchange email addresses. I promise to email him soon and often; but then I stop myself. Is he okay reading English? He says he has a friend who can help him, so don't worry about that. He signals for a taxi to send me back. We hug warmly and say *sawadee* with prayer hands under our noses. I give him a peck on the cheek. And then, from a back space in my mind, I ask him a last question: "Joe, are you gay?" He smiles, but it's a thinner, a more thoughtful smile than I've seen from him. Before I duck into the taxi, Joe replies, "Maybe. Not sure."

On the short taxi back to my hotel, heart beating fast and stupidly getting ahead of myself, I'm already trying to project the "what next?" from this brief but headlong and heady time I've just had with Joe. The future, I grant, is fuzzy. Only one thing is at all clear to me: how much I really like this guy. As to his final answer to me just moments ago, now feeling about thirty years younger thanks to being with him, I interpret "Maybe. Not sure." as a "Yes."

TO BE (GAY), OR NOT TO BE

"Gay guys bond differently than straight guys do."

Among the many tread-worn stereotypes straight men and boys love to stick it to gay guys, is their predictable, unnatural effeminateness. The pansy effect. Even in the third decade of the twenty-first century, it would not be shocking to overhear such a bar conversation among manly men. One that derides some "obviously gay" guy's walk, hand and finger movements, speaking cadence, or (the sure giveaway) choice of clothes and accessories. I confess to having held a similar stereotypical attitude in my younger adult years, though I honestly cannot recall vocalizing it to any extent.

I mean to say that, while I may not have found effeminate men off-putting or a subject of derision, my perception, for a long while, was that most gays look and act noticeably different. That they act—no offense— like pansies. This attitude underwent a shift somewhere between my early thirties and early fifties. In those two decades, unbeknownst to me consciously, I must have been moving along that SO Continuum Joseph informed me about—toward the far left, that is.

How I eventually, instinctively realize that not all gay guys are pansies is by, what else, examining what I see reflected every day in the mirror. I'm referring to the way I **am**, naturally. My demeanor, gestures, speaking tonality, how I carry myself, and yes, how I dress. It's all textbook, cookie-cutter straight! I don't know of a sissy bone in my body—not because I've so deftly kept some sissy side of me hidden. No, I wouldn't know how to act sissy if my life depended upon it. I do some online research and reading, enough to discover that there are probably just as many straight-acting gays in the world as there are effeminate-acting ones. And I further learn that there's even an accepted acronym for the former: SAG.

I bring this distinction—between SAG and SIS—up now because on the jet-lagging, twenty-four-hour excursion home, much of my waking time is devoted to the question of Joe's gayness, and why that should even matter to me at this point. Let's say first, that while I detect some innocent sweetness in Joe's disposition and manner of speaking, the overriding impression he presents is about as straight as Brad Pitt. Put another way, you could understand why any girl he might meet would ask for his mobile number.

On the one hand, his apparent straightness makes me

perfectly comfortable in his company. He acts like me and therefore easily blends into a straight crowd, rather than in any way screams GAY! For a "new gay" like me, who's still living—and working—in a virtually 100% straight world, being seen with Joe conveniently poses little threat of discovery. On the other hand, though, what I long for desperately right now is, if not yet a gay boyfriend, then at least a gay close friend. How am I ever to know *how* to be gay if I have no gay friends, no gay relationships with whom to interrelate? All of which brings me back to, not so much a conviction, as a wistful hope—that Joe just might become my close (straight-acting!) gay friend. Maybe more.

In debating and wishing for Joe's gayness, a realization comes to me that matters a lot more: the one whose gayness needs affirming most isn't Joe's, it's mine. My intimacy with Joe has gone beyond physical satisfaction to an emotional opening, sharing feelings of doubt about myself with another guy, which is something altogether new for me. As such, it has brought me a long way from my "once in a lifetime aberration, must never happen again" sexual encounter in Malaysia. And so, it's happening pretty much instinctively: I'm coming out within. No, I haven't declared this outwardly yet. But recall how I answered Joe when he asked if my family knows I'm gay: "I don't know if I am, but I must be." These thoughts sit in my head as I return home and prepare to visit my counselor, Joseph, for the second time.

I drive to Joseph's office, a week or so after my return from Bangkok. Not surprisingly, I'm in a talkative mood, excited even. I'm eager to share with him how my thinking has progressed since we first talked—importantly, that I **am** more accepting of my gayness. This means not only that, though true, I only want to have sex with men. It also means that I long for a relationship with another younger gay guy. Beyond relating these unfolding developments, I'm keen (maybe even a bit giddy) to spill everything about my time in Bangkok with a different Joseph—a Joe I'm suddenly damn attracted to.

Comfortably seated once again across each other, smiling, Joseph asks me, "How are you feeling?" I believe this is a fairly standard way many counselors initiate conversations with their clients. But I also assume that the question implies more than a perfunctory, "How's it going?" He wants to know, first and foremost, what emotions, attitudes, and issues (if any) I've been carrying around and contemplating—especially relative to where we left off over three weeks ago. I tell him, and hope he can read it in my face as well, that I'm feeling really good, much different than when we first met. More relaxed, more confident, more content with myself. And I hasten to add that my time in Thailand, more specifically with a certain someone I met in Bangkok, has spurred this "feeling good" feeling I have right now. Naturally, Joseph asks me to relate my Bangkok adventure in more detail.

I start by backtracking to that very first-ever trip I

made to Bangkok. The one where about all I remember is drooling inside a taxi over the sexy-handsome young Thai guys just about everywhere I looked. I had not had the chance to mention my seemingly innate "Thai attraction" to Joseph in our first session together. As an explanation for the drooling, I even joke about my American colleague's comment some years ago that I must have been Thai in a previous life. But then I shrug my shoulders and confess that, truly, I have no idea where this mostly physical-sexual affinity for young Asian guys comes from. Joseph, as I will find, prefers to listen a lot more than speak. He interrupts me here though, to state and to ask, "It's hard to pin down where our individual sexual attractions come from. As with straight people, some gay men are attracted to those nearer their own age; others are attracted to those younger. It doesn't matter unless the age-thing bothers you. *Does* it trouble you at all that you're, apparently, only interested in younger gay guys?"

Honestly, I don't know. Given my fifty-something years, am I troubled by my intense attraction to twenty-something men? *Should I be?* Of course I've thought about it. How could I not, when my two sons in their late twenties are already older than someone like Joe? I mean, if and when I do choose to come out to my adult sons, how am I ever going to spin that one? But beyond this, sure, I'm also vaguely aware of the stereotypical attitudes about December-May relationships, particularly among gays. "Oh, so you're a 'sugar daddy?'"; "Isn't it hard to *really* believe a sexy young guy finds *you* sexy?"; and, most distressing of all; "Just how young, exactly, do you like guys?" So, in answer to Joseph's question: yes, I do find attitudes like these disturbing. But if I were to find the right younger guy, and if I could tell he really did care for me, then I would think, "why not?"

Joseph nods and smiles again, as if to say, "Sounds all right." And then, "So, please go on, let's get back to your gay Thai friend, Joe—how you met and what he's like." I start with the obvious, how incredibly handsome and sexy Joe looks, especially featuring an alluring smile that would stand out in any Chippendales line-up. Furthermore, I believe it's that smile that conveys a beguiling kind of charisma unexpected in someone of Joe's twenty-two years. Next, I summarize Joe's Esan vis a vis Chinese Thai heritage. I then explain just a bit (I know only that much) about *Muay Thai* boxing and how Joe was trained in it as a boy to eventually become a teenage champion. I also note that he retains the washboard stomach and muscled torso of a teenage athlete. Finally, I spell out what I've learned about boy massage clubs in Bangkok and about HIS, where Joe and I met and where he earns his living. Oh yes, I also somewhat tastefully replay the highlights of showtime—gym swings and all—at the Boys of Bangkok.

Momentarily recalling that night so vividly—not the show, but those last few minutes together, and that parting question I put to Joe—my talkativeness falters.

Joseph, brows furrowed, noticing some change in my facial animation, pipes up. "What?" he asks. To which I say, "Nothing, really, it's just that as I was so sadly saying goodbye, for some reason I asked Joe if he was gay. His reply was, 'Maybe, not sure.'" I admit to Joseph that this question, including its answer and why the hell I even asked it in the first place, have been on my mind ever since.

Ever the counselor, Joseph rightly asks next, "Why *did* you ask the question? Does it matter?" In terms of my sexual attraction to Joe, as well as my attraction simply to being in his company, I concede whether or not he is actually gay matters little. But as I'm coming to realize I'm gay at fifty and not fifteen, I feel woefully unprepared and inexperienced entering a gay world—with the one I've chosen dominated by younger gay guys. Not to mention that I haven't got a single gay friend in the entire universe. So, something *does* matter. Maybe it's this: making up for years of lost time, I'm in a hurry to **be** gay, to feel what it's like to **live** gay, and what I need more than anything else right now is a gay someone to help be and live that way, or at least get started.

I've already alluded to Joseph's preference for listening over talking. He again breaks his listening silence here to offer some perspective. First, he tells me he's glad I may have found a first gay friend, a younger one at that. To which he right away adds that, in his practice, he has encountered many older guys like me—baby boomers, that is—who also have taken a good long time to figure out (or, more aptly, *choose* to figure out) they're gay. And a fair number of these also find themselves attracted to younger guys. Joseph's sly way of endorsing that sign on his waiting room door, that, not to worry, what I'm experiencing is rather "normal." Further, he offers some credible rationale for this phenomenon: gays and bisexual guys born in the nineteen-fifties were really caught in a squeeze-time. Yes, the sexual revolution got rolling in the next decade, but it was a movement that primarily favored straight men and women, not gays. The latter pretty much had to continue doing what they had always done—not merely keep the truth hidden, but do whatever was necessary to convey the opposite. To act and appear normally straight. As a case in point, Joseph reminds me that, back then, we all thought that movie-idol Rock Hudson was the prototypical guy's guy; until we learned in the 1980's why he was dying of AIDS.

But, Joseph clearly empathizes with my urgency to live as a gay man, which he describes as much more than experiencing gay sex—to enjoying the fullness of gay intimacy. That, he claims, involves my being capable of opening myself totally to another guy. To share dreams and doubts, private desires, and private fears with another man. Yet this is not, in his experience with most other guys like me who have been living as if straight for years (and, especially those who have been married many of those years), something that usually comes naturally—or happens quickly. To which he recommends I go slowly, as best I can.

Then, much as he did in our first session, when informing me about the SO Continuum, Joseph offers yet another important Gay 101 concept: "Gay guys bond differently than straight guys do." He brings this up now, he says, because it obviously pertains to my questioning of Joe's gayness. While Joseph agrees that, for now, having just met and not knowing with certainty when Joe and I might be together again, there's no reason to think too much or stress out about whether he's gay or straight. See what develops. But, *if* over time I find myself falling for Joe and *if* he's straight, then that "enjoying the fullness of gay intimacy" Joseph advocates is not going to happen with him. Curious for more, I press Joseph for further detail about this bonding difference between gay men and straight men. He confesses, reluctantly, "To really understand how gay guys bond together—especially in an intimate boyfriend kind of relationship—you have to get into one, go through one. Talking about it doesn't come close to feeling the simpatico of it all."

Glancing at my watch, I see our time is once again running short. But there's one other aspect of my new-found friendship with Joe, beyond our thirty-year age difference, beyond the question of his "SO," that I'm wondering about—what he does for a living. Though I'm unfamiliar as of now with the common street-term for what Joe does, I'll eventually overhear it often around the sois of Silom: "money boy." As mentioned, I've informed Joseph about massage for men clubs in Bangkok, how I first met Joe at HIS, where with so many sexy young guys in one place, you become the kid in the candy store. But even in the candy store, everything has a price. So, without directly asking Joseph for what he thinks about my potentially "first, close gay friend" expecting to be tipped handsomely for his time with me, I suppose I'm fishing for, at least, a "no big deal."

Joseph puts down his pad of paper, tugs at his glasses as if thinking before responding too quickly. I already know that he prefers opinions about my attitudes and behaviors to come from me, not him. But he smiles and, per usual, places his response in the context of the gay world. He acknowledges that pick-up gay bars, massage lounges, and saunas have been staple venues in the gay culture since forever. So for any gay guy, me included, to frequent one is not unusual. No big deal. But, he adds, while some of these venues involve pay for sex, in the Western world, most do not. Either way, as he has observed from years in his practice and from personal experiences himself, it's extraordinarily uncommon for two guys to meet up in places such as these and subsequently become close friends; and almost unimaginable for them to become boyfriends. I make no response other than to gently nod my head up and down, signifying "Got it."

As we wrap up, I book another appointment for next week. I don't know exactly what I want to talk about then, I just know I want to keep talking—probably further about this "pay for sex" complication, among others. As we're scribbling date and time, Joseph asks about my plans to keep communicating with Joe and whether I might see him again before long. I note that I've got some work coming up a few weeks ahead in Hong Kong, and that I'm considering asking Joe if he would like to meet me there afterwards for a few days together. In the meantime, we've exchanged email addresses and I've already sent him one, thanking him for good times and, sure, saying I miss him. I've also been thinking about stopping in at the downtown Thai Passion restaurant; there are some young Thai waitresses there, and I'm wondering if I could hire one of them to translate my emails to Joe into Thai.

Driving home, my mood is less exuberant than when I set out, but by no means am I in a downer. I mean, even with the age thing, the gay-straight thing, and the pay for sex thing, I'm still really, really attracted to Joe. I'm thinking, a helluva time in my life for puppy love! Yet, around the periphery of this indulged excitement, some questions linger: What kind of "gay bonding" might I actually experience? What meaningful gay *relationship* could ever be possible for me—with a straight money boy? Not to sound despondent, but I'm pretty sure you can't pay your way to gay.

TAKING CARE
"About 2 million baht."

A few days after my session with Joseph, I follow through with my proposed visit to the popular downtown Thai Passion restaurant. I arrive mid-afternoon, on purpose—to seek out a potential Thai waitress-interpreter between the typically crowded lunch and dinner servings. I've eaten here two or three times, but I cannot say that I remember anyone who works here. I just know the staff is largely comprised of bilingual Thai-English speakers. All appears quiet, as I expected upon entering. I'm greeted shortly by a smiling, middle-aged, Thai-looking woman who tells me, unfortunately, they aren't currently serving again until 5 p.m. I nod my head and explain that I'm not here to eat. Rather, I'm looking for a Thai-English speaker who might be interested in, for a fee, translating my English emails into Thai. I quickly add that I have a close friend in Bangkok with whom I have begun corresponding via email, but that I want to be able to express myself as clearly as I can. My Bangkok friend understands spoken English somewhat, but cannot read it, relying on a friend to translate what I send aloud into Thai. Now my Thai maître d' nods her head back at me and says, "Oh, sure, I think you should speak to my daughter, Tiya, who also works here. Let me call her out."

As she approaches me from the kitchen doorway, I find I'm charmed once again by that distinctive "Land of Smiles" look that seems only to emanate from Thai faces. Wanting to make a good impression, I make the traditional Thai prayer hands beneath my chin and politely say, *"Sawadee, Krup, Khun Tiya."* At this, Tiya returns the greeting with an ever-broader grin—a look of happy surprise really—and exclaims, in clear American English, "Oh, so you speak Thai!" Slightly embarrassed by her undue compliment, I joke that she just heard the extent of the Thai I speak. I go on to explain that because I have a Thai friend in Bangkok with whom I plan to communicate regularly via email, I'm looking for someone whom I could hire to translate my English emails into Thai. Might she be interested? (And I hasten to add that I'm willing to pay, say, fifty dollars per email, or some other hourly rate that she thinks fair.)

While she's plenty busy working full-time here, Tiya says she's open to doing a trial run. I'm to email her a typical-length email and let her see how long it takes to complete the translation. I insist she takes at least fifty dollars up-front as a kind of starter-retainer. Throughout our getting-to-know-each-other conversation, I'm struck by the similarity of her eager, innocent enthusiasm and welcoming smile with that of Joe's. I comment that her personality reminds me so much of my Thai friend, at which she asks (probably expecting my friend to be female), "What's your friend's name?" I tell her his name is Joe, and for some strange reason, mention right after that he's twenty-two. Tiya, eyebrows arched in surprise, exclaims, "That's my age too!" Maybe the similarity I sense isn't merely a coincidence. For now though, it seems Tiya has all the information she needs from me and will await my first Joe email to her inbox. In the not too distant future, however, Tiya will find herself needing to ask me—ever so bashfully—just how close a friend Joe is to me. The more intimate the "friendship," the more colloquially different the words she must choose for the Thai translation.

I've already sent Joe several emails since returning home. Keeping the conversation going with my one and only gay friend seems the ostensible reason for emailing every other day or so. But then there's my need for communication and an understanding companionship, which has never been greater. For one thing, I'm living straight-as-usual again; of course, with my wife of thirty-plus years, but also with my daily work. This means most waking hours are spent in calls and emails between me and my long-distance business partner in Chicago and among our various scattered clients. All of whom are

1000% straight. For another, my mind and heart as well, remain preoccupied with imaginings: Who is Joe to me? Who might Joe become to me? When can I see him again? Such daydreams, call them fantasies even, have set upon me way too fast (Christ, I've known Joe for what, a week?). But then, my immersion into gayness has been so long in coming, that it is no wonder this later-in-life hurry-up shows. More than anything, though, what movies keep playing in my mind are those "trailers" featuring, near-ecstatic happiness—during both intimate sex *and* intimate conversation.

Regarding conversation, namely the one I'm aiming to keep open via emails, Joe has held up his end. I've received two email responses from him, in understandable, if ungrammatical at times, English. No doubt why each one of his is considerably shorter than the ones I send him. True, the voice I hear in the emails sounds only here and there like Joe's; but then, as he said he would do, he has asked a friend who can write English passably well to draft his replies. Nevertheless, it's a warm, soothing voice I hear. It encourages me to relax as much as possible, not to overthink things, not to rush big decisions, and to please come back to see him soon. As I read and re-read Joe's sweet words, I'm struck by the thought that, just maybe, his English translator is female. This impression strikes me foremost in the more than friendly way each email ends: "Love, Joe."

To be clear, as teenage excitable as I may be, I resist

reading too much future hope into these tender email signatures. Instead, I focus on my more immediate desire: finagling a way to get me and Joe back together. I had been thinking of asking him to meet me in Hong Kong, right after my work there about three weeks hence. But, in talking with Joe via phone about this, I learn he has no Thai passport, and although acquiring one in Bangkok isn't difficult, I detect some apprehension. Joe's not accustomed to flying internationally, let alone solo to a bustling, Cantonese and English-speaking place like Hong Kong for the first time. Joe wonders if, instead, I might fly to Bangkok after my work; or better yet, meet him at Don Muang Airport (in Bangkok) and fly on together to, say, Phuket. Though I've heard much about Patong Beach in Phuket—particularly the area surrounding the famous Paradise Hotel, which while not the center of the gay universe, probably comes in a close second—I've never had the pleasure. So, naturally, I love Joe's idea. But what I love most has nothing to do with Patong Beach or the Paradise Hotel. No, what I'm grinning from ear to ear about is the chance to spend two or three nights in a cool hotel alone with Joe. A chance to, at the very least, pretend we're a couple!

The trip to Phuket finally happens, but not without a discombobulating, frantic start. I've taken Joe up on his plan to meet up at the Bangkok airport. I've also purchased his e-ticket online. All he needs to do is taxi to Dan Muang, check in, go through security, and wait for me at the boarding gate. As for me, upon arrival from Hong Kong, since I'm not entering Thailand until Phuket immigration, I expect to walk from my arriving flight to the Phuket flight gate. What could be simpler? Almost anything else, it turns out. Because I've only ever entered Thailand in Bangkok, I'm unaware that I must go to a transfer waiting area until being bussed out to the Phuket-bound plane sitting, not at a terminal-attached gate, but out on the tarmac. Once I've spoken to the transfer area agent, it's clear Joe won't see me at the normal Phuket boarding gate, nor will I see him here. We will only meet up at our plane seats. Our very first private trip together, with a shimmering white, brand new, boutique hotel waiting for us at a tucked-away spot toward the very end of Patong Beach. There is also the thrill of flying Thai Airways down there together. Suddenly, I've got some queasy insides, which in short order will turn into accelerated anxiety.

I find I cannot speed-dial Joe's mobile fast enough. Or often enough. You see, this waiting area is below ground and, well, I have nary a signal. What's worse, I cannot leave the transfer "cell" because, obviously, I've not been stamped into Thailand yet. Calls, texts, even email attempts, but nothing. As boarding time nears, I'm certain Joe is at the domestic boarding gate, and no doubt wondering where in the hell I am. My only hope is that, surely, he'll take the bus ride from his gate out to the plane like me, and we'll reunite there. But that's not what happens—at all. Thinking about it now, of course I would do what Joe does—standby for a later Phuket flight while waiting for the must-be delayed arrival from Hong Kong. No way, if I were Joe, would I risk getting on a flight to Phuket and finding no Mike. What if something happened and Mike's not coming at all?

Needless to say, the hour-fifteen flight to Phuket is sheer misery for me. How can I stop wondering and worrying about what Joe must be thinking, especially with absolutely no word from me? Upon landing—at a place I've never been before either—I'm stunned to discover that the airport is a good hour's drive to beachy Phuket. Of course, even before I'm through immigration and into baggage claim, I'm feverishly poking my cell trying to reach Joe. It seems now his phone is either out of charge or switched off. In the hired taxi and as hyped up as I can ever recall, I finally get through, but before I can say anything at all, Joe asks where am I? I tell him Phuket, to which, in a high-pitched voice I've never heard from him before he shrieks, "WHAT! PHUKET?" He is still at Don Muang Airport and has been waiting there at least three hours. Given that even in normal phone conversations we struggle to make meanings clear (why I have opted for emails instead), with both of us upset and for sure confused, I beg him to wait there just awhile longer, until I get to the hotel. Someone there who speaks our two languages well will help us figure out how to get him to Phuket—soon.

It isn't until around 2 a.m. that Joe finally arrives at our secluded and, now that I've seen it, romantically appointed Patong Beach hotel. After checking in and finding a staff member who can speak with Joe, things start to get sorted out. Joe can catch the last flight out. I even send a private hotel car to await him at the distant Phuket airport. I've calmed down somewhat once I know Joe has landed and been picked up. But as we bear-hug with a much relieved *sawadee krup* in the lobby, where I've been waiting for him, I say, "I need a drink." This, then, is how building our eventual, closer relationship really gets going, I believe. In the grand scheme of things, some definitely small drama. Nonetheless, this early shared panic becomes something we both feel, remember long, and many times in the future, laugh about. After all the mayhem of just getting here together, the next three days go smoothly; for me, more like heavenly. We do Phuket day and night: beach, fresh seafood, and mostly gay bars. But the heavenly parts for me happen in our cool, big balconied, ocean-view hotel room. After play, we talk (and drink) long, each night into the wee hours. We talk family, worries, things we're proud of and some we're not, and dreams for the future. I talk a lot about not understanding how or why I became gay so late in life, and more sadly, what unbearable pain revealing it will inflict upon my wife and sons. Joe listens and does his best to calm me. This gives me pause: I've got a professional counselor named Joseph aiming to help me at home; perhaps I have a freelance counselor named Joe doing the same for me here. Something odd though, especially at these moments when I'm sharing my fears for the future, watching Joe nod and smile empathetically, I imagine not so much a potential boyfriend, as another son.

Move ahead in time some. Over the next nine to twelve months, I'm able—either with on-site workshops or thanks to some in nearby Asian cities—to get to Bangkok a few times. More and more, though, these times are insufficient. I'm not able to get the "couples time" I'm looking for unless we go away someplace. So, we do. There's a trip, at last, to Hong Kong. And it's a damn fun trip too, guiding Joe around for his first time in China. We take the Star Ferry back and forth from Kowloon to HK Island; ride the double-decker from there to Stanley; take the near vertical tram (at night, of course) to Victoria Peak; learn the right way to enjoy Peking duck—scallions and plum sauce; and bar-hop at night around Wan Chai, where one wild-ass night Joe coaxes me into a go-go bar. We are serviced by dozens of barely-eighteen looking, pole-dancing Filipino girls.

Against my better judgment, we order drinks for a few—the ones already squeezing themselves into our booth and getting snuggly on our laps. These girls don't ask Joe for his cell number, but they pay every bit the same attention to him that the girls in Bangkok do. And, as in Bangkok, Joe's doesn't mind one bit. In fact, four or five Filipino girls have asked him—us—to go out with them to some smaller, local live-music bars they know. I'm unsure, suspicious even. But I can read in Joe's face how much he's enjoying the alcohol and the girls. He's ready. I'm ready too—for whatever it takes to make Joe happy. So, off we go. It is only after somehow stumbling back in one piece to the hotel near sun-up and then waking with hangovers around noon do we discover the "no way!" shock of how much I spent last night (sorting through ATM withdrawal and credit card signature slips jammed in my wallet). Right around 2,000. That would be U.S., not Hong Kong, dollars. Privately, in the madness of this realization, I look into myself again: Am I trying to pay my way to be gay? If so, at this rate, I haven't money enough to get me there.

Luckily, my next trip with Joe ends up costing me only hundreds, not thousands. I'm in Bangkok again for work. Having known Joe now for about six months, and with a few free days remaining before heading back to the U.S., Joe would like to drive me home—his home, that is, in Bua Yai. He wants me to meet his large family, especially Hong, his older sister/surrogate mom, whom I've heard much about. But mainly, he wants me to experience farm life in Esan for the first time. The trip could not be more opposite to our Hong Kong trip as it goes slow and easy. No bars, no go-go girls. Just super-spicy food, boxes and boxes of Leo beer, and family—lots and lots of Joe's family. Everyone wants to welcome me and speak with me, but my Thai fluency remains embarrassingly nonexistent.

So I rely on smiling a lot, nodding my head in thanks, and every so often, asking Joe to attempt some translating of his brothers' and sisters' and cousins' Esan into rough English. It turns out one middle-aged cousin was once married to an American guy. She speaks English rather well, and I welcome the chance to converse with someone, anyone. Only one thing she asks me during our chat do I still recall, however: "Does Joe have a girlfriend in Bangkok?" On the seven-hour ride back to Bangkok, this question—to which I know of no answer—rattles around in my mind, along with a related one that I ask myself: I wonder who Joe's family thinks I am? Probably *not* Joe's boyfriend, I'm thinking.

Soon I'm at the twelve-month point with Joe, having come some distance in my relationship with this guy I first met smiling brightest within a crush of smiling massage boys. I'm taking stock of where we are, of where I am as a gay guy. (I should say, more correctly, I'm perpetually taking stock of these two things.) Joe and I have travelled and slept in hotels together; watched *Muay Thai* boxing live at Lumpini—way too many times, for me; bar-hopped with Filipino bar girls; gone late-night disco clubbing (with HIS friends); and Joe has even taken me home to "meet the family." He remains my only young Thai friend, perhaps also my only gay friend. I say "perhaps" for obvious reasons: First, I haven't repeated that question about his sexual orientation. The one I asked following our first night out at Boys of Bangkok, so we're still at "maybe gay." Second, while I can see he enjoys my male company, he clearly enjoys female company, namely the young sexy type, as well. As I've observed from day one, Joe is straight-acting, like me; and I prefer to assume that makes him a SAG, like me. For now, anyway, Joe is helping me with my ever-so-slowly evolving initiation as a gay guy, whether he's gay or not.

In those weeks and months when Joe and I aren't spending a few days together in Bangkok or elsewhere, he works at HIS and I cities in and out of the U.S. Our exchanging emails continue. Tiya's translations have worked beautifully, so our arrangement proceeds. Somewhere around about my fifth or sixth email to Joe, as I stop by the restaurant to pay her some cash, Tiya finally musters the courage, very politely I should add, to ask if . . . well . . . um . . . might Joe be more than just a close friend? Of course, she sees my private thoughts to him—such as, how and when am I going to tell my family about me; such as, how much fun I have with him when we're sharing a hotel room in Phuket. Being born Thai, Tiya has no problem with any LGBTQ types, no doubt counts some in Thailand among her friends already. She just wants to use the right Thai words and expressions, particularly for conveying important feelings like, "Love from my heart, Mike."

Emails aren't the only missives I'm sending fairly often. In the first few months, knowing Joe isn't always making big tips at HIS and that he regularly wires a good portion of what baht he makes to family, like Hong, back in Bua Yai, I choose to help him out some financially. Call it a goodness of the heart thing in me, but also call it one tangible way to keep showing Joe that I want to be more than another customer to him. That I really do care for him. Ironic, huh? Offering more money so as **not** to be thought of as a customer.

That word "care." Given the global presence the English language enjoys, Thai—much like other non-English tongues—carries some well-known, oft-used English expressions. One I've heard from time to time in Bangkok is "taking care." As the two words are commonly used in the U.S., the U.K., and other English-speaking countries, telling someone to "take care" usually means "stay well" or "be good to yourself." Or, if in conversation we mention that we're "taking care" of a new baby or an ailing grandmother, it normally means we're literally helping them with their daily, bodily needs. But in Thai, especially when spoken within gay Thai circles, "taking care" has a quite different connotation. Foreign guys with young Thai boyfriends (many of whom come from rural Esan to work in Bangkok) "take care" of those boyfriends by regularly sending them cash—to cover costs of living in expensive Bangkok *and* to send back to their immediate families up in the Northeast. Taking care, you see, typically involves more than just one's boyfriend. Among the other missives I send Joe, then, at least during those first months, are—harebrained at it sounds—one-hundred-dollar bills packed in FedEx envelopes and delivered in Joe's name to, of all places, HIS Massage. This mode of money transfer doesn't last long, however. Once other HIS boys, even front desk manager types, understand that these odd deliveries (come on, what else would FedEx *ever* deliver to a gay massage club?) contain crisp Ben Franklin's, there's no guarantee Joe ever gets his hands on them. So, Joe suggests the security of wiring monies from my bank to his, which after providing me the wiring details, begins . . . and goes on, and on.

Over the next year or so, other sidebar trips happen, inside Thailand to Chang Mai and Pattaya, and one in particular outside of Thailand, to Ho Chi Minh City—again, after my client work there in Vietnam. This one becomes the singular, most eventful trip I ever take with Joe. Other than the prevalence of so many classic Vietnamese street stalls and garden-style restaurants, all serving up delectable, freshly made spring rolls among other dishes, Ho Chi Minh offers visitors nothing special. Even less so for gay visitors. Central HCM City sports barely a handful of gay bars, all rather tame. For a country located so near Thailand, it's gay friendliness couldn't be farther away. And it's palpable. When Joe and I walk the city's heart, around the opera house, groups of idle men selling from carts or just squatting on haunches smoking, give us long, disgusted looks. Part of this I get right away—Joe, looking pure Thai to me but Southeast Asian to people here, easily passes for a young Vietnamese guy (in fact, when we go out, store clerks and restaurant servers all address him in Vietnamese). That automatically makes me the old Western faggot who's taking advantage of innocent young Viet boys. We even draw similar scandalous looks while boarding lifts inside the Caravel Hotel.

No big deal. We aim to find The Apocalypse Bar, which bills itself as the city's number one rocking nightspot, attracting mostly straights, but also gays. Plus, the world-renowned Saigon Bar sits atop the Caravel itself, with a hot Filipino band playing every night of the week. And so, our first two nights go textbook, out until places close, and then back in our room drinking the mini-bar dry, playing on the bed, and—as always with Joe—engaging in really soothing conversations about our families and ourselves. Oh, and sleeping late. In fact, by the time we awaken each morning, we have long missed the breakfast included in the price of our room. Fortunately, sitting kitty-corner from the hotel is a decent bakery-café. We've made it there the last two days and here we sit again on our last full day, waiting for our morning coffee and eggs around 3 p.m. Joe's quieter this morning than usual. I ask if he's feeling OK or, maybe, still recovering from many whiskies and loud nights. He says there's something he has been meaning to ask me, but he has been a bit too shy to ask it. I respond with some of his own advice to me, "Joe, don't think too much. What is it?"

We're still passing back and forth that Thai-English dictionary I bought, but our times together along with emails have made our mutual understandings easier. Joe has an opportunity to get out of the boy massage business, to join up with another young Thai in Bangkok who has started a gold jewelry business—to become his partner. The small company makes items that the majority of Thai's value and purchase most: reasonably affordable 14K gold bracelets and necklaces. There's a small craft-by-hand factory outside of Bangkok which Joe has visited a number of times. The workmanship is fine; Joe happens to have one of their necklaces in his pocket to show me. I'm impressed feeling its lightness in my fingers, noticing the simple details. It's attractive, casual, not at all showy. And unisex in style. Such a necklace sells at retail for around 6,000 baht (about $200). The big BUT, though—what Joe has been shy to tell me about—is the obvious: to become a partner he must invest. His proposed partner needs more capital to buy more raw gold and purchase additional gold smelters. More than almost anything, I want to see Joe out of the massage-sex business, for selfish reasons but also because I have long believed his obvious street-smarts cleverness warrant him a chance at something better. Ideally, sometime in the future, his own small business. So, though surprised somewhat by this news, I'm open to helping make that happen, if I possibly can.

    I ask the obvious, how much do you need to invest? With the look on his face a cross between a wince and a smile, Joe replies, "About 2 million baht." Thinking, at first, I've misunderstood (not unusual for me), I inquire again, "Howww much?" Joe repeats the amount. I'm still not mentally quick with exchange rate calculations, especially when I get to the bigger numbers. But I know instantly we're not talking a few FedEx Ben Franklin's here. Joe's talking big bucks. On the spot, I'm dazed, stunned, stupefied—all those "are you kidding me?" reactions. And something else, I see Joe moving his lips, telling me some other related details, but almost as if a grenade exploded within earshot of me, I momentarily only hear a ringing in my ears. Joe sees at once that I'm in shock. He does what he is normally quite good at with me, especially when anything the least bit upsetting happens. He smiles and urges me to relax, not worry too much. And he quickly adds, "Mike, just something I want you to think about. When we get back to Bangkok, I will take you to meet my partner and to see the factory. Then you can decide for yourself."

Flying back to Bangkok with Joe, my mind tries in vain to balance my heartfelt desire to do *anything* I possibly can to show Joe how much he means to me, against the bare-ass facts—two million baht, or fifty-thousand dollars at the current exchange rate, is plainly infeasible. Five thousand, maybe. But fifty? Unthinkable. Insane. But another thought overrides even this tussle in my head. Another question, rather: Just how far must I go—am I *willing* to go—to take care of Joe?

TRUTH, AND CONSEQUENCES
"Oh, my God. You're gay!"

There's a part of the story I'm not telling. Don't want to tell, really. A part that's too embarrassing. No, too humiliating. But, unfortunately, for purposes of advancing my story, it's time I reveal this up-to-now hidden episode. It's essential if I'm to credibly dramatize the family dilemma overshadowing me in choosing to be gay. I use that verb "dramatize" intentionally. For in a life mostly devoid of drama, I'm about to come unhinged amidst it. Rather than moving ahead in time, I need to move back to that window comprising a few weeks after my very first gay encounter—that one with Vincent in Malaysia. To be more precise, what I need to relate happens between my confessional meeting with Father Tom but before my initial visit to HIS, and Joe, in Bangkok. And what I need to relate, but would still prefer not to, shares something deceptively in common with that confessional meeting.

Around ten days after my time with Vincent, undressing for a morning shower at home, I stop cold at what I see reflected in the mirror: large, irregularly shaped red blotches appear all over my chest, stomach, rib cage, back and buttocks. A never-before seen rash of some kind, but with no pain or itch accompanying it, just bright crimson amoeba shapes everywhere. My wife, approaching her sink, stops, also stunned by the mirror's image. She asks something like, "What in the world have you gotten into? Or eaten that you shouldn't have?" We're both well aware of my, often in years past, serious allergies to pollens and some foods. I stammer back that I have no earthly idea what this rash is, nor its source. Since it seems painless and I'm not scratching, we do the sensible thing—agree to wait a day or two and see if it goes away. It does, within forty-eight hours. Yet, while the rash disappears from my body, determining its likely cause refuses to disappear from my mind. My instantaneous first suspect: I've picked up some kind of STD from Vincent. Online searches at sites like WebMD, however, lead me to a much more sinister suspect. This unusually shaped, torso extensive, cherry red rash (typically occurring within two weeks of exposure) is a common symptom of initial HIV infection.

Panicked is much too mild a word for my mental state. Something between that and suicidal would be more apt. First-off, quite naturally, I'm in denial: we had safe sex anyway . . . didn't we? (We did.) Then I'm clicking from website to website, certain there must be dozens of medical conditions with rash symptoms similar to mine. There aren't. And even if there were, what IF, as unlikely as it must be, I have been infected? One next step is patently obvious—I must get tested ASAP. Articles about HIV, though, all indicate that since the virus may take up to 12 weeks from rash to detection, one needs to undergo testing a second time at the twelve-week point. Then there's that *other* next step. However unlikely the outcome, my wife must learn of my possible infection, also ASAP.

If I had already been dreading and delaying the day when I would finally tell her I'm gay (which I have nowhere near the conviction or courage to do at this point in my barely begun gayness), this news immediately takes over my psyche as the preeminent breach in our thirty-year relationship. Clearly, with my orientation having gravitated towards gay—for months, if not over a few years—the intimacy in our relationship has declined, but not disappeared entirely. Even if it had, though, our underlying love and respect for each other demand the truthfulness we've always shared. Our long years of mutual care absolutely require full disclosure in any situation where one of us puts the other in potential danger. So, I'm both compelled but also resolved to tell all. Well, not exactly all. As I'm by no means man enough now to say I'm pretty sure or I think I may be gay, I need some plausible pretext to explain my urgency in seeking HIV testing. Though I'm much embarrassed to admit it, such a pretext exists—the one I initially peddled to Father Tom. Didn't work out so well with him; but it's my *only* option right now with my wife.

I spin that story then, very much along the lines I already rehearsed with Father Tom: one long, international trip after another; lonely and drinking more than I normally do many evenings; approached by a young, sexy Thai thing (woman, that is) for an in-room massage—not ever imagining what all it would turn into; finally, not something I could ever live down or be proud of, nor ever want to happen again. Yet one more gender-deception to mask and delay my choosing to come out gay. This time, though, accompanied by many mea culpa's. I don't need to belabor her reactions. They're as one would expect: the shock, the sadness, the utter disappointment, but also (what I read in her eyes) the underlying disbelief. After all, we know each other pretty darn well after thirty years and two adult sons. Not to mention that neither of us has ever shown an even modest interest in another mate. Nevertheless, there is no disagreement on getting into my GP's office—today if possible—to start the testing protocol.

The subsequent twelve weeks are expectedly tense. The rift I've cleaved between us will eventually feel less raw, especially when that second test proves me to be HIV negative. But as self-loathsome as I feel during these days and weeks, for all the pain I've off-loaded on my wife, I also come to realize that the day for coming out gay to her—and to my sons—must be much, much sooner rather than later. Because, besides this painfully wounding gunshot I've discharged, there's that other little matter of my growing attachment to Joe.

By the time we receive an all-clear from the HIV scare, I have known Joe for almost three months. And we've made that first, frantic trip together to Phuket. Emails and FedEx envelopes are also in transit. At home, while relief from the negative blood test has eased tensions some, nothing feels settled. While I cannot read my wife's inner thoughts, her demeanor says that something about this whole affair doesn't add up. During these days when I'm not traveling for work, I therefore find my need for counsel with Joseph greater than ever.

I schedule sessions with Joseph weekly, sometimes twice per week. I never mention the HIV business; it's too debasing for me to admit, even in the presence of someone who undoubtedly has heard a lot worse. No need anyway because Joseph knows of my inner struggles toward eventually coming out to my wife. One visit stands out, one for which I've retained the hand-written one-page set of notes I prepared in advance. Though jotted down in bullets, and in no particular order, looking them over again now, years later, they portray a faithful likeness of the *truths* confronting me: truths that I must know will out, but am not yet ready to act upon. Here are those notes, verbatim (which I've for some reason entitled atop the page "Bangkok—Afterwards"):

- *I've not lived my life like this—ever (The Big Lie).*
- *What I'm doing is simply wrong (as in Right from Wrong).*
- *My self-esteem falls.*
- *I cannot figure out who Joe is to me—friend, boyfriend, son?*
- *I feel like I'm falling into an impossible relationship with him.*
- *I love the way I feel in Bangkok—totally alone as Me, at HIS, out and about with Joe; kidding around, touching, laughing; I can't wait to get back.*
- *If I were single (or even separated, living by myself), I'd go every few months.*
- *But where could it possibly lead, end?*
- *I know that what I experience in Bangkok is pure fantasy—it cannot become my life.*

In my opening explanation "About the Title: *Choosing To Be Gay*," I state there are hundreds of reasons for someone whose gayness remains hidden to disbelieve, deny, and delay his choice to come out. Looking back on these notes, I'm struck with another big reason not to choose to be openly gay: too much doubt that, once chosen, happiness could ever follow. What doubt, specifically? Relationship doubt: that I can say goodbye to a loving, thirty-year relationship with my wife and lifetime best friend; and surviving that, that I can actually attain an intimate, loving, gay relationship with Joe (or with *any* young guy). Lacking confidence in either of these two, I continue my counseling conversations with Joseph over the next couple of months. And while I cannot recall the particulars of those conversations, I do remember my resolve to come out to my family finally reaching the tipping point.

It's holiday time, Christmas approaching. I'm with Joseph for the last time of the year. As soon as I settle into my usual sofa seat, I pronounce that I'm ready to come out to my wife and sons. In fact, I tell him, if it were not for Christmas season, when we're all wishing to be family happy, I would do it today. Not prone to giving me behavioral advice, though well-aware of how distressed I've been living a lie at home, Joseph nevertheless speaks up. He gets that I must come out to my family, if for no other reason than the inner relief he knows will follow. But, he adds, it would be devastating if my imminent timing was based solely upon the hope that a lasting, loving gay relationship with Joe would follow—which might, or might not, happen.

I tell Joseph I know he's right. I also assure him that my timing has nothing to do with what may or may not come to pass with Joe in Thailand. It has only to do with salvaging my self-esteem. That shadow of self-hatred that immediately followed my first-ever gay experience has turned into a permanent darkness—mind, heart, and soul. Then, there's that ever-present age thing that refuses to leave me alone: over fifty and dreaming of a relationship with a younger guy, any chances of my being even remotely attractive fly past me at light speed. Whatever time I have left, I need it all now. I need the freedom to discover what possible, loving gay life I might someday have. And the only place to seek that freedom resides within my family. I set my next appointment with Joseph for mid-January, but he most kindly offers to see me at any time—especially should I wish to revisit my coming out decision—before then.

It's a bit odd that I cannot remember the exact day I approached my wife, what with that day becoming such a momentous one for both of us. An anniversary to be excused forgetting. It was during that first week in the year, after all the New Year's hubbub. I'm pretty sure our family holiday times came across as quite normal to our sons, friends, and neighbors. But between us, that underlying tension, many months after my bizarre infidelity story, never seems to have stopped simmering. Other than to cover subjects like household care, outdoor exercise, shopping, upcoming family events, the day-to-day stuff, we don't talk much. So, little wonder that when I interrupt her quietly reading, saying something like, "There's something I need to tell you," what I get back at once is, "Oh no. What now?" Along with an accompanying grimace that says, "I think I'm going to be sick."

It's funny what kinds of things you pray for in life—even funnier how, when you least expect it, the prayers get answered. Throughout a good part of my adulthood, along with the normal prayerful requests for health and happiness among family and close friends, I have consistently asked for the gift of courage. Character mettle I never felt I had enough of. I'm pretty sure the kind of courage I imagined receiving from above would manifest itself in, say, those life-telling moments, those situations demanding one stand up for a right principle, especially if in doing so one were to risk losing friends and reputation. Only a long while after this moment of truth with my wife will it dawn upon me that, in this very instance, my prayers were being answered. I muster the courage to speak the truth. About the sex massage I say, "Everything I told you was true, except for one thing. The person giving me the massage was a young man, not a young woman." Yes, word for word the same ending to the same lie I first told Father Tom (and another barbed reminder that, sooner or later, there's no escaping the truth).

"OH, MY GOD. YOU'RE GAY!" This, her primal response—with a face contorted in frightful pain. A look I avert my eyes from, yet a look never to escape from. I reply in barely a whisper, "Yes, I think so." Seconds go by, feeling more like minutes. The seismic shock needs absorbing. But then, as in nature, a second wave. She blurts out—an alarm I've not anticipated at all but grasp at once: "Oh no! I've not worked. What am I going to do?" In the changing of that one little noun, from sex with a young *woman* to sex with a young *man*, I realize I've cheated my wife out of her husband *and* her lifestyle. There's a blur, probably in self-preservation, regarding much of who says what next. Only I know I tell her immediately and emphatically that, whatever we decide about our marriage, we will *always* share whatever I earn fifty-fifty. I make this pledge under no guise of nobility; it's simply what's right. To make sure she believes me (after all, I have lied once before), I say we'll find a lawyer and pen a "post-nuptial" agreement, making the earnings-sharing pledge legal. Then silence. Out of words, we each need some time alone. As I leave the house to take a long, long walk and reassess this coming out choice I've just let loose, she calls after me, "You need to tell the boys—soon."

I've said little so far about my two sons. As they're both grown and no longer living at home, up to now they have remained on the sidelines of my coming out dramas. I surmise further that neither has any idea of the underlying stress, going on for a while now, within their parents' home. I'm so very proud of them, have been all their lives. More to the point, I know how proud they are of me. So, although I've gained some minimal measure of relief in coming out to their mom, I'm by no means home-free. That twice-told, bogus story about some sex massage "mistake" on one of my trips to Asia cannot possibly be spun to them. Their mom may have reacted, momentarily, with disbelief; but I'm fairly certain their disbelief will not pass quickly. Each has only known dad as perfectly straight (I'm a SAG, don't forget). Virtually stymied by their pride in me and their constant assumption of my straightness, my mind remains blank: what **do** I say, how **do** I tell them? Surely not something like, "Hey, by the way, there's something rather surprising I've been wanting to tell you—I'm gay."

I ask to meet with each of them separately, telling them I have something I must talk to them about. I quickly add that, "No one has died, no one is seriously ill, and no one is getting divorced." That last piece, of course, is only true at the moment; though in fairness, neither my wife nor I has any idea at this point what will become of our marriage. Face-to-face with each of my boys, I opt for the only thing that makes sense—just say it, "I'm gay," followed by some vague timeline of how this change in sexual orientation seems to have come about. Each listens, closely, in silence. As is often common with male children, no tears are shed, just some mix of comforting and concerned looks. My younger son, after hearing me out for ten minutes or so, makes the ordeal bearable when he says, "I just want you and mom to be happy. As long as we all still love each other, I'll be okay." Many, many times in the months and years ahead, I will recall the caveat in my younger son's words: how I treat my wife, their mom, and how she treats me makes or breaks things being "okay" for my sons. I do one more thing. A few days after speaking with them, I send each son a handwritten note, the thrust of which is to assure them, I'm still me.

It's generally believed (and definitely to be hoped

for) that, soon after coming out to one's closest family members, one receives an adrenalin-like dose of relief. I admit to experiencing some such relief, though I find it short-lived. Too much uncertainty about the future swirls—regarding my marriage, naturally, but suddenly more pressing is my relationship with Joe. I've come out to my family. I'm free; or certainly, freer to be with him than ever before. Within only a few days, then, I send him an email. A tell-all about my coming out to wife and sons along with the obvious expectation of an eventual divorce. Tiya translates and sends this email pronto, per my request. To my surprise, I get an email reply almost as fast—not something Joe routinely does. His English-translating friend expresses Joe's shock perfectly. He even uses all-caps in writing, "WHAT? YOU WILL LEAVE YOUR WIFE?" The email reply isn't long, but in reading and re-reading it there can be no mistake that Joe is unsettled by this news. He never expected something as dramatic as this. As I read between the lines, I believe I'm faintly hearing (accompanied by a sinking feeling in my gut) Joe say, "Mike, please tell me you are not getting divorced on my account."

FUTURE BOY

"I can't be your everything."

As it turns out, my coming out to family coincides roughly with a follow-on business trip to Asia. But not just another business trip, because this is the one for clients in Vietnam, Ho Chi Minh City to be precise. More critically for me, however, it's also that singular, eventful trip I'm ever to take with Joe—the one with the trip-ending, SURPRISE!, two-million-baht price tag. By this time, I've known Joe for over a year. During the intervening couple of weeks between receiving his implied email plea "please don't divorce your wife on my account," and our reuniting in Ho Chi Minh, I have not only emailed him back with reassurances, but also called him a few times. I guarantee him that telling my family I'm gay, along with the probable separation from my wife to come, are only due to me: to help me once again, maybe, start living with myself, start *liking* myself. Joe's relieved, I think.

As I board planes westward toward Vietnam, anticipating the joys of being with him again (and freer than ever), I struggle to accept a long-unfolding reality. Joe likes me, a lot. He also needs me, a lot. But, as hard as I find it to suspend my disbelief, Joe likely has no desire, nor intention, to become my boyfriend, let alone, somewhere down the line, my partner-husband. In fact, within another few months I'll discover that Joe is *incapable* of being either of these persons to me.

About the gold business, and the big baht, big bucks investment for Joe to become a partner in one, once we're back in Bangkok (together, right after Ho Chi Minh) he does indeed take me to meet his would-be partner and to see their would-be, jointly-owned, necklace and bracelet factory. How can I best convey my impressions, my gut reactions to being introduced to the potential gold business-partner and his factory operation? I think the most apt expression I could use would be that I feel genuinely sick to my stomach. Putting aside for the moment the absurdity of the thousands of dollars Joe—and even more so this partner—are seeking, I know instantaneously, upon looking Khun Partner in the eyes that he is never to be trusted. His eyes dart everywhere, never once looking directly at me as we initially *sawadee krup* each other. Reading a guy's honesty or true intentions from his eyes sounds stereotypical, but never have alarm bells rung louder in my head than they do now. As for the operation itself, as we walk among lanes of connected, metal assembly tables, in temperatures somewhere north of 95 degrees, where young men pound and shape soft gold by hand, nothing could be more obvious: these workers are nearly all teenagers, many younger than eighteen. Though I've heard about youth sweat-shops throughout Southeast Asia, this is my first ever witnessing of one. When we leave the factory, I quite literally stagger out, breathless, into the bright of day.

Joe asks me if I'm okay; he can see that I'm not looking so well—perhaps the intense heat inside? I tell him I'm going to live, just shocked (I use the Thai word for shocked, *tok jai*) at how young the workers are and at the poor working conditions. I add quickly that he and I need to go back to the hotel to talk, and drink. The partner guy grabs Joe by the arm and leaves Joe with a few curt words. Though I can guess what he tells Joe, I ask him to translate. It was something like "If you want to be my partner, I need to know. Now." In American business slang what he was really telling Joe was more like, "I want your investment money—yesterday."

Joe drives us back to my hotel in his Isuzu pick-up—the one for which he personally saved two-hundred and fifty thousand baht (while working at HIS before we met) to use as a down payment. I don't say much. Though he desperately would like to know what I'm thinking about moving ahead with the gold business, he instead does most of the talking while driving. He tells me that his older brother, Vichai, whom I've come to know and like, would co-manage his half of the partnership with him. He itemizes what material rewards the current owner-partner enjoys from his successful gold sales so far—his new Toyota Fortuner SUV, his new house, his Tagheuer watch, and very-latest Nokia mobile phone. Joe does this not so much because he is envious, but to further my confidence in the inevitability of his own financial success. Running a gold jewelry factory appears much more than ascending from employee to employer, it's upgrading from occasional fifty to one-hundred-dollar tips to an on-going stream of substantial capital. Joe doesn't add this last part, but he implies it when he insists that he intends to pay me back—over time, that is.

I'm half-listening. Mind numb. Yet, I **am** thinking—what though? Like anyone with even a jot of common sense, I'm dead-certain that handing over roughly fifty-thousand dollars to get Joe into a gold factory/sweat shop must be the craziest idea, business or otherwise, I've ever confronted. Such was my first impression days ago when Joe first verbalized it to me in Ho Chi Minh city. Today's on-site images have only magnified, amplified, and redoubled that original impression. So, the decision is crystal-clear: "Joe, I'm so sorry but I cannot help you with this." Or, should I say, this *would be* the crystal-clear decision if only my head were in control of the decision-making process. But it's not. My heart (cleverer than the limbic brain even knows) exploits the following arguments in overriding all logic:

I've cut myself off from my rest-of-life partner, my wife . . .

I have no idea how long it will take for my sons to fully be okay with their (surprise!) gay dad . . .

I have zero gay friends (still), let alone a bona fide gay boyfriend . . .

Whether Joe is that boyfriend or not, he has been wonderfully kind to me, especially when I needed someone to listen, to credibly care . . .

Above all these things, I love Joe. Even if in exactly what context I'm unsure, and—if there is any way I possibly can—I want to help him have a chance for a better future.

Once back in the hotel lobby bar, sharing a couple of Johnnie Walker Black and sodas, I tell Joe, "Look, I know next to nothing about the gold jewelry business, in Thailand or anywhere else. I see gold shops all over Bangkok—you and I have been to and bought at some—and I know how Thai people own gold not just for show, but for future value. If you and Vichai think you can make a go of it as a wholesaler to gold shops, I'll help you . . . IF you're 100% sure about your partner." With a smile broader than I've seen from him in long while, Joe reminds me that he has actually known his new partner for a few years. They worked together briefly at HIS, before the partner himself found some customer to pay his way out of massage and into gold. Joe's sure. I only wish I were.

I can't recall ever moving or wiring fifty-thousand dollars anywhere (and definitely not to anyone), so I'm unsure how best to proceed. But, aiming for some measure of control over such a hefty sum, I tell Joe we ought to open a Mike-Joe joint account at Bangkok Bank, which stands as a Bank of America equivalent in terms of size and reputation within Thailand. I also make clear that it will take some time—after my return to the U.S.—to round up those funds and get them deposited, but we can open our account before I return home, tomorrow in fact.

When we meet that next morning at the Bangkok Bank on Silom, I'm more than a little surprised to see Joe's new partner tagging along. Of course, by now, I'm used to Joe's family and friends turning up, unannounced to me, at dinners and bars; but this guy's appearance throws me. More alarm bells in my head. Joe asks me to relax. His new partner merely wants to take an "advance" on Joe's initial investment so he can buy some urgently needed new equipment. So, upon completing the paperwork and depositing around two-thousand dollars (sixty-five thousand baht), Joe promptly withdraws all but five-thousand baht and hands it over. The gold business partnership is underway. Joe is all smiles, and me, though not even midday, I'm once again needing a drink.

Over the next few months, bundles of baht wired

ahead, the gold sales seem to go well. And, when I return to Bangkok after an absence of two months, Joe is happier than I've ever known him to be. He proudly declares he and Vichai are beginning to make some good money. It's way too early for me to ask approximately when he and his brother might start putting some of those profits back into our joint account—something, by the way, I'm not counting a great deal on anyway. However, if for no other reason than to sustain my confidence in and comfort with the whole deal, Joe volunteers that he remains steadfastly committed to "saving" some of their profits in our shared account soon.

As for our personal relationship, it remains kind, caring, and with usual intimacy, both physical and conversational. Perhaps better said, not much has changed. With such a magnanimous gift of hope—for him (and me?), was I expecting some change? Some uptick in our standing with one another? The stereotypical, expected, sugar-daddy answer to this question has to be, "Yes, of course! I take better care of you; you take better care of me." Looking backwards, these many years later, I honestly don't believe I was looking for or even hoping for some kind of stronger commitment from Joe to me. I believe I only wanted two outcomes: to keep on keeping on with Joe—still my only young, sexually intimate, Thai friend; and to make Joe happy, with high optimism for some better future than if I had never come along. If, back then, I wondered at all about why our relationship remained (as Thai's often say in English) same-same, the day before I'm to return home again, I learn that I needn't wonder ever again.

It's a Sunday and Joe has agreed to meet me at my service-condo around 11 a.m. My U.S. return flight leaves mid-morning tomorrow. As is our routine on most days in Bangkok, we meet for lunch, go bowling or play snooker, hang out at the condo, sometimes see a movie at the mall, and go out to some bars—usually with Joe's HIS crew—at night. And, as is typically routine for me on my leaving-tomorrow last day, my emotions comprise a mix of excitement at having one more full day with Joe and sadness at having only one more full day left with Joe.

It's around noon and Joe's a no-show. I dial his number, but get only v-mail. Another hour, more calls but no pick-ups. My anxiety level rises hour-by-hour, revolving around worry that something unexpected has happened—an accident maybe—and around the steadily diminishing hours I have left to enjoy on this Thai trip. It must be around 4–5 p.m. when Joe lightly raps on the door, never having called. Though I'm distraught, beside myself with hurt feelings, I'm not angry. I just want to understand and so I ask, "Where have you been? I've been waiting for you all day . . . and you never even called." Sheepishly, Joe apologizes. His body language says he would rather not explain, but he obviously concludes the time has come: "Mike, I'm sorry, but I had to spend time today with Mem." I know of Mem, a girl whom, using my mobile phone, he has spoken to in soft whispers every time we have traveled out of Thailand. And though I've never inquired about who Mem is to him, on a few occasions he has referred to her fondly. About all I know at the moment is that, like Joe, she is from Esan and he has known her long. By now, I'm crying. All I can think to say back is the obvious: "But, Joe, this is my last day with you for a while, and you promised to spend it with me."

Joe asks, "Can we please sit down?" Looking me dead-straight, Joe speaks the necessary truth I now know we have both chosen to circumvent: "Mike, I can't be your everything. Mem is my wife."

Have I taken a gut-punch? Had the wind been knocked out of me? Am I shell-shocked, gob-smacked? None of the above, more like heartbroken. Did I know Joe is not gay but straight, not my boyfriend but some young woman's husband? Well, as to Joe's being gay, I've alluded to my lingering doubts already. Aside from that evasive "maybe, not sure" answer to my long-ago question and his dependable straight-acting behavior, there have been other signals along the way. For example, never did we speak of ourselves as "boyfriends," despite appearing that way to others when together in public. Even more telling, we have never, ever kissed. It seems odd saying this now because, of course, gay couples who love each other kiss just as straight couples who love each other do. But, considering that Joe is, as straight Thai guys like to say, "not gay but a man"; and considering that I am, at best, a novice gay who for decades believed he was straight and who up to this time has never had even one gay relationship, the fact that Joe and I have never kissed speaks volumes.

As to hearing of Joe's being married, I confess I'm at least somewhat surprised to learn. I mean, sure, I know he likes girls and they like him. I also know, from those very first visits to HIS, that many straight guys work in the gay sex business, perform as gay escorts. Nearly all have girlfriends, wives, and mistresses outside of their day (or, more probably, night) jobs. And, as I eventually come to understand, these girlfriends and wives typically look the other way when their boyfriends or mates are entertaining, massaging, and having sex with gays—the money that comes in is just too good for the couple to forgo. Begrudgingly, I suppose I could ask, "Joe, why have you never told me you were married?" But then, in fairness, he might just as well ask me, "Mike, why have you never asked?" Up to a point, don't ask don't tell has served us both well. If nothing else, though, hearing Joe has a wife explains perfectly why he was so distressed when I emailed him about my pending divorce: a husband already, he was in no position to ever become mine.

I cry some more. We mumble things. Always kind to me and never in any way heartless, Joe hates hurting my feelings in this way. I can see this in the pained look on his face. Finally reaching some level of calm, I know of only one way forward. I ask Joe for help. More a plea than anything else: "Joe, please, please, help me find a good guy—a good **gay** guy—to maybe become my boyfriend." Putting his arms around my shoulders, Joe promises to help me meet some gay Thai's. He knows of one or two working at HIS whom he says are good-hearted and honest. He'll introduce me to them. But not wanting to disillusion me yet again, he whispers something like, "Mike, please don't get your hopes too high. Young gay Thai's—especially the sexy ones working in Bangkok—are looking for young Thai boyfriends, not older farangs." Joe's words of caution will stick with me for years, but not merely due to his genuinely good intentions in protecting me from further boyfriend disappointment. Joe is Thai, Joe is young, and Joe is sexy. But Joe *isn't* gay (made official just now). Joe's words of warning will stay with me because I find that, among some young gay Thai's, there are exceptions to "Joe's Thai boyfriend rule." Totally unbeknownst to me at this heartbreak point, I'm destined to become one of those exceptions.

Crushed, but recovering little-by-little from today's real-life soap opera episode, I want to go out, get some fresh air, eat something (I've spent all day waiting, not eating), and definitely, drink some whiskey. Joe is game, of course. He suggests that to make the most of the time we have left tonight, we return to the Boy Soi, where we first witnessed that wild-ass Boys of Bangkok show but have rarely visited since. He knows of another bar, further down into the soi that has become, so he's heard, the number one popular bar. It's called Future Boys.

Arriving at the entrance around 9:30 p.m., Future Boy's popularity is plainly evident. It **is** a weekend night, but even on weekends, seeing a bar nearly full of customers this early is unusual. The best remaining seats are the ones forming a facing-perimeter around the rectangular stage, so we end up quite close to the Future Boys themselves. As was the norm at Boys of Bangkok, in the hour or two before showtime, all boys must stand and rotate clockwise (moving every minute or so) around the stage—aiming to attract customers sitting, drinking, and either looking for a boy to take out or, more commonly, waiting for the show to begin. Joe orders beers. Me? I'm once again mesmerized by the sheer number of beautifully handsome, slim but well-defined, young Thai guys in rotation before me. It reminds me of that first visit to HIS massage, only here there must be three or four times as many amazing looking boys. And there's no end to those seductive Thai smiles.

It might seem that, confronted once again with such an abundance of Thai eye-candy, I would be getting over the grief of today's events—that I would be excited, even, to be out in a gay bar again. I'm neither of these. Watching boy after boy go by, drinking disinterestedly, but really, feeling very little. Joe and I make small talk; what else is there to say to each other? Of course, we still care about each other, and want to continue being together when

I'm here, despite that elephant-in-the-room third person: Mike's invisible, TBD gay boyfriend. Oddly enough, regardless of this mindless funk I'm in, one of the rotating boys—number 19—catches my attention. Much as when I zeroed in on Joe among the HIS crowd, for some unexplained reason, this young guy seems to be looking right at me. He's not just handsome, but stunningly so. High cheek bones, a la Joe; classically squared facial features; slim but lightly muscled V-shaped body. And, among so many gleaming smiles, one that somehow calls out to me.

Joe misses very little. He quickly picks up on my intermittent gaze towards number 19. He asks, "Mike, do you want me to call him over?" As engaged as my eyes have been on this young guy, I'm inexplicably nervous, daisy shy, tongue-tied. I have no earthly idea what I would say to any bar boy invited to sit and drink with us. So, instantly, I plead with Joe to hold off: "Please, no!" Thirty minutes pass and the show is starting. Lights go dim, naked boys carrying candles climb the stage—a typical opening show in the soi, with hot wax dripped upon their bare chests. I need to hit the toilet, located just a few yards away over Joe's left shoulder. As I reach the restroom door, I pass by number 19 who happens to be standing nearby with a few of his bar buddies. He smiles warmly, and I return the smile. When I come out, number 19 remains next to the door, and as I pass him by, I feel him gently, ever so lightly, run his index finger across my back, across my shoulders. And I hear him laugh.

No sooner do I sit down again, reaching for my beer, than I look over Joe's shoulder to see number 19 still looking at me with that indelible smile. My confidence suddenly aroused, I say to Joe, "Let's call him over." Joe signals him and he sits between Joe and me. Naturally, he offers a polite *sawadee, krup* to each of us. He speaks first to Joe, in Thai, but then I notice they quickly switch to Esan (though I speak very little Thai and no Esan, being with Joe all these months, I've learned to detect Esan words from Thai words). So, number 19 is Esan; same as Joe. Hmmm . . . No wonder I picked him out from such a large crowd. I ask his name. He replies, in perfectly clear English, "My name is Ball, which in Thai is pronounced Bon. Like Footbon or Basketbon." I tell him my name. So surprised to hear a young Thai speaking English with such clarity, I then ask him, "So you speak English?" To which he says, "Yes, I do—but not very well." Typical Thai modesty. Hearing only a few words and phrases, I know at once that Bon speaks English much better than any other Thai I've met. There's something else that I detect, though, in Bon's manner of speaking. It's that subtle sound of higher education. And I ask if he has been to college. He has—two years.

Whatever happens on stage with the show, I have no recollection. I'm captivated, enthralled, fascinated with this beautiful—no handsome; no both—guy sitting so close to me, talking with me easily, and just being so damn nice. Not much time passes when, out of the blue,

I ask Bon, "Would you like a customer tonight?" My transformation from daisy shy and tongue-tied to "let's go somewhere private together" is astonishingly swift. Without hesitation Bon smiles, "sure," and gets up to go change from his Future Boys bikini into street clothes. Once back, I pay the bar, both for our drinks and the privilege of taking out a Future Boy. Just outside in the soi, Joe and I bear-hug and I kiss him on the cheek. I assure him I'll call and email as soon as I get home, and aim to be back again soon. As Joe heads towards Surawong Road to catch a taxi (back to his apartment with Mem), Bon turns me in the opposite direction. There's a pay-by-the-hour hotel hidden in the shadows at the soi's end, well positioned for the regular boy-customer nightly clientele. But before we begin walking away from Future Boys, I have one more question for Bon: "You're gay, right?" No hedging to my question this time as Bon flash-smiles and affirms, "Yes, I'm gay."

Our time at the parking meter hotel is brief and a bit awkward in the beginning. But not at all unpleasant. While undressing to shower, upon lifting my shirt Bon says, "Mike, you have a nice body." Not a compliment I've ever heard from another guy, but definitely one that pleases, coming from an honest-to-goodness, stallion attractive gay guy. We share tidbits about our families. I tell Bon I've been married, have two adult sons, and only realized I was gay a couple of years ago. As it's our first time and getting past midnight, I tell Bon I had best go back to my hotel—I have to leave first thing in the morning. He walks me toward the taxis. All the way I'm wishing I could stay one more night, have just a bit more time to get to know this sweet, intelligent dreamboy better—I mean, we can actually converse in English, no dictionary required. At the taxi, I ask for his email address, which he writes down for me. I promise to email him soon, and he kisses me lightly on the lips. Does he truly expect to hear from me again? No doubt, working in the boy bar, he has heard such talk from customers before. But the last thing he says makes me think he *does* expect more: "Mike, please come back to Bangkok soon. I want to see you again."

Taxiing to the hotel, I'm reliving the past six to eight hours. Could it really be that, in such a nanosecond of life, I've gone from begging Joe to help me find a gay boyfriend to actually meeting my first young gay guy who is, no shit, too good to be true? I guess what I'm really wondering is, could there be any way—at all—that Bon might be a part my future?

THE LIGHT TOUCH

"I'm not gay, but my boyfriend is."

It's not possible for me to overstate the significance, or overlook the ripples emanating still, from that singular moment when in Future Boys, with an innocent gesture as I pass him by, Bon traces his finger ever so lightly across my upper back—and laughs. I say this because this first-ever physical connection with Bon, in the form of a feather-light finger touch, will for years to come prove emblematic of Bon's personality. He is Esan, like Joe. He is drop-dead handsome, like Joe. But in personality, he could not be more different from Joe. Whereas Joe is outgoing, often outspoken, and charismatic, Bon is reserved, quiet, and self-effacing; a personality of a much lighter shade. In these ways, though only just turned twenty-three, Bon's personality could not be more like my own. They say that opposites attract. But they also say that likes attract. After, what, only two or three hours knowing him, and while making the long flights home, I'm absorbed in my attraction to Bon: his looks, his amazing-sexy smile, his ability to easily converse with me, his intelligence, and that first glimpse at his diffident but easy-going personality. Oh, and that other thing—obviously, he comes across as openly, comfortably, and happily gay.

No wonder, then, that as soon as I'm back in the States, I'm eagerly planning a return-to-Bangkok visit; this time not so much a HIS visit, but a Future Boys one. Of course I want to see Joe. But beginning to think that, somehow, Buddha just might be involved in my miraculous introduction to Bon on that very same day I lose Joe to Mem, I'm hasty. I aim to take advantage of Buddha's intercession (if that's what it was) before he has a chance to take it back. Much as when I first met Joe, upon returning home I waste little time in sending Bon an "I hope you remember me" email. Actually, I recall little of that first email's contents, but the gist remains with me: simply to tell Bon how much I like him, despite such a short "first-time" together, and that I hope he likes me too. One other thing I absolutely remember wishing for—that, with future Bangkok times spent together, he might come to think of me as less a customer and more a friend. Not an unfamiliar wish on my part.

With Bon's relative fluency both speaking and writing English, two big changes in my Thai emailing occur: I have no need of Tiya's translations when writing him; and, better still, the number and regularity of emails between me and him rachet up considerably versus those between Joe and me. Having just barely met before parting forthwith that night in Bangkok, these early emails contain little beyond talk of work (me in and out of the U.S.; Bon at the bar), talk of family, and talk of weather. But, for me, they serve to sustain the spark Bon lit in me. And, within a few weeks, I'm able to tell him of my upcoming return visit to Thailand. Bon emails me back right away about his excitement, looking forward to seeing me again soon. That's all I need to hear to put aside the reality that I know only too well: working in Future Boys every night, Bon has every opportunity for some excitement as new customers come and go. Yet during this upcoming trip, I'll not only learn a great deal more about just how cool and sweet-hearted this young guy is; I'll also learn how very unhappy he is having to work in a gay bar.

There's that boutique hotel. Joe pointed it out to me on our very first snooker outing. The Silom Serene. He knows the woman who manages it there and, he assures me, the rooms are nice and quite reasonably priced, with staff that are mostly English-capable and friendly. Best of all, Silom Serene sits no more than two-hundred meters off Silom on Soi Pi Phat, putting it well within my favorite "center of the gay universe" Bangkok neighborhood. As a smaller local hotel, it also offers a convenience not always available at the Marriott's and Meridien's of the city: outside "guests" can be admitted to your room at any hour (with your permission). No ID's need be held at the front desk, no questions need be asked. Seeking out a home-base near to Future Boys with easy come-and-go access for Bon is paramount for my first-ever return visit to him—to enable as much time as possible getting to know each other a whole lot better.

Upon arriving at Don Muang Airport, Joe picks me up in his Isuzu and drives me to the hotel, where I've booked one of their suite-rooms. I chose the suite-room based upon their website photos, illustrating a full kitchenette, living room area, large separate bedroom and bath with a large tub and shower. Oh yes, and a king-sized bed. My planning isn't all that elaborate, though. I'm just wanting to ensure an ice-cold fridge to hold plenty of jumbo Heineken bottles (Bon's preferred beer), a comfy living room sofa to sit, drink, and talk until we get too tired, and a large enough shower and bed for the two of us. Bon knows of my expected arrival time at the hotel (in fact, he knows of the hotel as well, perhaps having once or twice popped by with some guy he's met at Future Boys). He will meet up with Joe and me to initiate what will become—for the next few years—our routine: the threesome meets for dinner, a bar or two after, usually some entertainment after that, and then we split up for the remainder of the night. Joe goes to the apartment he shares with Mem, while Bon and I go to our hotel home-base.

About this threesome thing, and that it rolls on as long as it eventually does, I think a great deal. Not so much at the time it's all happening, but often in the years since it has ended. Clearly, looking back, I'm in a kind of no man's land; I mean, literally. As I arrive to meet up with Bon for only the second time, I have no man in my life. Hell, I still have no gays in my life! Already out with my family and handful of close friends for nearly a year, I have spent less than six hours of my life in the presence of another gay guy. Am I gay? Really? Okay, Joe and I have engaged in incidental male sex for nearly two years, but he's not gay and has a wife with whom he is regularly intimate. In the hindsight of years, this gay Mike + straight Joe + gay Bon togetherness seems a lot less bizarre than it might have at first. Not so much here in the beginning where I'm in transition, being sort of handed off from my straight "faux boyfriend" to my potentially TBD gay boyfriend. But later, when I find my abiding gratitude to Joe—for all the kindness, care, and calm he gave me at the lowest time in my life—precludes me from pushing Joe out. No way can I imagine saying, "Thanks for everything, Joe. Especially for introducing me to my dream boy, Bon. See you in the next life."

The funny thing is that, in these early becoming acquainted days with Bon, he himself wonders who this Esan guy, Joe, is to me. Bon knows instantly, when he first sees me with Joe at Future Boys, that Joe is straight (some 6th sense—like the converse of gaydar). Me, he's a little less sure of. He tells me later, during our first night at Silom Serene, that upon first seeing me, though I act straight, I'm likely gay. Why else would I be in a gay bar? Plus, it's not that unusual to see gay farangs and their straight Thai boyfriends in the bar. So, while downing one Heineken after another in our Serene room, we replay that night of a couple months back when we met at Future Boys. Though nothing is said directly, Bon is subtly inquiring if Joe and I might be boyfriends. By the same token, as I ask Bon about his customers at the bar, I'm subtly inquiring if he has a customer-boyfriend—someone "taking care" of him. To my veiled question, Bon answers straight away: no.

In fact, Bon goes on to talk at length about how much he detests working in a gay bar. He's naturally shy, and though speaking English better than most, he's no conversationalist. The bar is so competitive—there are many cool, sexy boys much more outgoing and therefore more popular than he. But above all, the pressure each night to have quick sex with customers is constantly distressing. As he puts it best, "Sex with many guys, one-night stands with strangers I'll never know or see again—that's not me. Not who I am, or who I want to be." But compared to other jobs he has had (restaurant waiter, factory worker), the money he can earn at Bangkok's number one gay boy bar cannot be beat. Bon, like so many other bar boys, has a Buddha-given responsibility to send money home to his farmer parents, brothers, and cousins in Esan, to, as he will tell me time and again, "lessen their burden."

I describe the intimacy that Joe and I have engaged

in during our roughly two years as friends as incidental "male sex," purposefully. Because until I meet Bon and he spends this first full night with me at Silom Serene, I never could imagine a distinction between male sex and gay sex. But now I know there is. It's a BIG distinction, and a wonderful one. Bon's youthful, easy, and sweet disposition—hell, his casual innocence in being gay—changes everything. He remains a master of the light touch as we hold each other so gently and kiss. Yes! Kiss. And then, at the height of things, in my mind this flash that remains with me to this day: "Oh, good God. **This is what it's supposed to be like!**" I'm not referring just to the pleasures, but to the emotions which cannot possibly be figments of my imagination: Bon's enjoying being with me as much as I'm enjoying being with him. In the corner of my mind, Counselor Joseph's words come back to me: "Gay guys bond differently than straight guys do." Seems I've come a long, long way from that stare-in-the-mirror, admission moment. No need now to keep convincing myself I'm gay.

How many times have I mentioned that, until this very moment, I had no gay friends? Ever since coming out to myself and then coming out to my family, I remain painfully aware of this gaping hole in my choosing to be gay. I've chosen to *accept* my gayness; I just have no idea how to go about *living* it. After fifty-plus years, I've pretty well mastered living straight. And with my ever-pulsing work and travel demands, then spending what other family time I have doing my damnedest to, as my younger son wished for, show that we all still love each other, my straight life brooks no interruption. Without the trips to Thailand and the occasional intimacy with Joe, there's nothing remotely gay going on in my life at all. I crave gay friends for the obvious, most basic of reasons: to learn what it's like becoming and living gay. My counselor, Joseph, may have given me the clinical definition of being gay, but I'm completely missing the experiential definition of being gay. I yearn to ask as many gay guys as I can, things like: When and how did you know for sure you were gay? Before you came out, what kind of gay life did you have? And when you came out to your family and friends, what was that like? How hard was that choice—to admit to yourself and to others?

Little wonder, then, that after my "gay sex" eureka moment on the bed, we adjourn to our living room sofa and talk, and talk, and talk. With non-stop Heinekens and some background Thai music on the room's CD player, I begin learning more about who this Bon person is. And, finally, I can ask someone who just might know the answers to my many living-gay questions. My recollection is that we end up talking until nearly sun-up. And though I have no ready quotes from all that we discussed, what stands out is just how much—in tight ties to our families—we both have in common.

Listening to Bon go on about his deeply held sense of responsibility to his parents and brothers impresses me.

I've read about this opposing notion between Asian and Western parents and their adult children. In Asia, adult children are expected to care for their parents, especially financially, as they become elderly. But in Western countries, especially the United States, the last thing parents want is to be dependent upon their adult children as they grow older and retire. But listening carefully to Bon, it's plainly evident that he regards contributing to the financial well-being of his mom and dad as not merely a cultural expectation. It's a measure of his own self-esteem. He repeats again his rationale for working where he does, to lessen his parents' burdens.

As I say, I'm much more interested as we talk through the night in listening and learning from him than I am in telling him my story. But I do tell him more about my wife and adult sons. And, as Bon listens to me, he too hears a sense of responsibility—one that I have in being kind to and taking care of my wife now and long after we will divorce. Bon tells me that he has never known a Western guy like me, married with grown kids; but he clearly grasps the responsibility I feel. The more we continue to know each other and build our relationship, the more we both will often note the significance of our families to the two of us, as a couple. No matter how much we might love each other, if it sometimes comes to a one-or-the-other choice, family must always come first.

For the rest of my time this trip, we spend every night like this one. We grow closer. Over the next few months,

I return a couple of times, each night paying Future Boys whatever is necessary to take Bon out for the night. With a few of his very cute gay friends from the bar (Whut, Jeab, and Nam—for whom I also pay the bar), we rotate different entertainments every night. Sometimes live song and dance venues, sometimes cavernous discos, sometimes intimate karaoke rooms, and sometimes just partying together in our Silom Serene home base. For me, despite passing the age of fifty-five, life in Bangkok runs fast, furious, and often in a blur. One thing is crystal clear, however. I'm falling in love with Bon. So, on one of these nights, on the bed around 3 a.m., and no doubt feeling the effects of some alcohol, I say the words: "I love you, Bon." He seems happy to hear this, though he doesn't repeat similar words back to me.

The next day, with Bon having returned to his apartment, I suddenly panic. Not because I lied, but because I fear I said too much too soon. I recall Bon telling me that he once had a Thai boyfriend, but not for very long. That guy told Bon many times, "I love you," but he played around secretly, until Bon found out and ended things. As Bon would tell me, "He was a butterfly I couldn't trust." So, I know Bon has been burned once already with those, sometimes too easily spoken, "I love you" words. When we meet up later, I need to talk. I apologize if confessing love to Bon upsets him, and I even take the words back, telling Bon something like, "Let's just say that I like you so very much, and we'll see how we *both* feel over time."

Bon's okay with this, with everything. And soon after I return home to the U.S., he sends me this email:

> Mike—Since I left my only boyfriend, no one ever said he loves me. Then last Friday night, you told me. That made me very happy. Though today I know it's not the truth. But I'm glad to hear it. Especially because the words come from you, Mike. Please don't worry about what you said to me. I understand you. Still we are friends, right?

It turns out that, while I was a bit quick on the draw in professing my love for Bon, by the time we know each other one year, we can both sincerely—and passionately—profess the "I-L-Y" words to each other. Some intervening events help to make that possible. For one thing, we take a couple of trips together out of Thailand. Ironically, our first trip is to Kuala Lumpur, the starting out point of my gay odyssey. Bon has some good Thai friends working in gay bars there, so we visit and party with them. Another trip takes us to Hong Kong, though nothing on this trip resembles the outlandish stuff I let happen that time with Joe. But most significant is Bon's escalating need to leave the bar, to get free from the shame of working there. For me, getting him free is even more vital: I can't stand sharing him, when I'm not there, with "customers."

Bon has long imagined owning a small shop, where he could sell artificial orchids that he makes by hand, from clay. Theses orchids are artistic, painstaking to mold and, especially, to make look and feel almost alive. After knowing Bon perhaps six months, he in fact gifts me with one of his creations. It is so well crafted that, when I carry it home on the plane, flight attendants compliment it. But the true test of his orchid facsimile work occurs as I pass through U.S. Customs. An officer pulls me aside to inspect my orchid of clay, thinking it is illegally alive. So, as we near the one-year point and the profess "I love you" point, he and I are making plans to open an orchid shop near his apartment, and to permanently take Future Boys out of Bon's—and my—future.

Not to be overlooked in our planning, though, is something else rather important that we agree to. We are officially boyfriends. To celebrate this announcement, I have an idea. Among the many joys of shopping in Bangkok are the endless street tables and booths selling any and all kinds of T-shirts—usually with funny, erotic, or profane expressions written on them. I'd say that my many times in Bangkok have by now taught me that that the T-shirt is the "national apparel" of Thailand. Anyway, the one T-shirt my eye has been on the most is the one I propose buying, in matched set, for Bon and me. It reads: "I'm not gay, but my boyfriend is." A humorous touch for what started out as a wonderfully light one.

THE RIGHT CHOICE

"Be gay. It's OK."

So, a young, jai di (very kind-hearted), gay Thai—a guy right out of my dreams—credulously tells me, a foreign guy thirty years his senior, that he wants to be with me. Freely uses the "B" word to address me. In the recesses of my aural memory, I cannot help hearing familiar, well-meaning voices, like Joseph's. They cautiously apprise me, "For two guys to meet up in places such as gay massage clubs and gay bars and go on to become boyfriends is not just uncommon, it's almost unimaginable." This followed closely by Joe's attempt at protecting me from further heartache when I ask his help in finding someone for me: "Mike, young, sexy gay Thai's want young Thai boyfriends, not older foreigners." Against the odds laid out by two people who know of what they speak and for whom I have real respect, I come out a winner. How can such things be? Only one answer ends up making sense—one that I will get to shortly. But first, consider the perspective from, say, an imaginary, objective observer. To someone watching my behaviors, all of them, from Vincent to Joe to Bon. I can envision and empathize with how preposterously unlikely where I'm ending up now must look.

Most conspicuous of all, there's that foolish pattern of payment I engage in. I pay Vincent as an evening escort, I pay Joe as a masseur, and I pay Bon to be one of his customers. In each case, this is my means of introduction. Then, upon my swift attraction to and closer friendship with Joe and Bon, I offer to help them each financially. This starts out as occasional FedEx deliveries but ends up as frequent bank-wire transfers. All this snowballs into chunks of significant capital—one, to make Joe a partner in a gold business, and another to enable Bon to pursue his dream and open his shop of orchids. Anyone silently watching me might rightly conclude (despite my earlier misgivings about "paying my way to gay") that I'm not just paying for sex. I'm paying for friendship—ultimately, for the hope of a gay relationship. There's painful truth in this conclusion. And I offer little by way of defense. Still, as an older, been-around-life's-track a few times, relatively successful businessman, and not totally unintelligent, I can't avoid asking myself: "What **was** I thinking?"

Though on more than one occasion Joe advised me "don't think too much," I never stopped thinking about what I was doing, where I might be going, and what it all said about me. Even in those most joyful and pleasurable moments of intimacy, the possibility of my being taken advantage of never completely escaped me. Looking back, I more and more believe what sustained me, what gave me hope, was this conviction: "I cannot win over a cool, young guy's true affection or heart through my looks, my sex appeal. Not going to happen. I have only one thing going for me that might win out—I can 'smother him with kindness.'" Lucky for me, and I'm certain due in large measure to the DNA of my parents, being ordinarily kind comes rather naturally. So, seeking a younger guy's affection—even emitting an uncommon kind of sex appeal—through routine kindness, becomes my approach. And, at the risk of sounding defensive, my true motivation. Though doling out baht after baht, often in large quantities, to either Joe or Bon can justifiably be construed as buying someone's affection or friendship, deep down, what I believe I'm trying to do is simply help two guys (and their families). Two guys whom I really, really like and care about. Fortunately, too, I'm gifted somewhat with the resources to do that.

If, to my imagined observer, my pattern of payment seems foolish, then my other evident pattern of seeking out only boys in the sex business must seem idiotic, even dangerous. Not only are such guys mainly uninterested in a lasting relationship with an old farang, a good many of them aren't in the best of long-term health. STD's and HIV are pretty prevalent among them. While not oblivious to either of these facts at the time, I prefer to overlook them. Maybe even pretend they likely won't apply to me. Later on, if someone were to ask me, "Why **did** you only try to meet gay guys in the sex business?" my honest answer would be that I had no idea where else to go. I mean, from that first ever, 1990's moment in Bangkok, drooling over young, sexy Thai men from the taxi's backseat, I know exactly to whom I'm magnetically attracted. Where else might I have the chance to casually see, talk with and get to know cool-looking young gays matching my attraction than in places like HIS or Future Boys? At the mall? A snooker parlor? At a *Muay Thai* boxing arena? I don't think so.

So, despite both Joe's admonitions, and consistently exhibiting foolish and idiotic behaviors, how **is** it that I end up now with this "amazing Thailand" boyfriend of mine. Bon gives the same answer to this question as me: Buddha. So absurdly unlikely we find it that a twenty-three-year-old farmer's son, a devout Buddhist from Northeast Thailand, meets up with a fifty-five-year-old realtor's son, a one-time devout Catholic from middle-USA, and they both fall for each other. The only explanation that possibly makes sense: destiny by Buddha.

Even accepting Buddha's role in our meeting up, getting a real, live Thai boyfriend is one thing. How do I go about keeping him? Or maybe a better-posed question is how do *we* go about keeping each other . . . building a long-lasting, loving relationship? Agreeing to become boyfriends is merely a first step. Come to think of it, a step that in gay Bangkok rarely leads to a long-lasting relationship. Both of us know too many stories of older foreigner/younger Thai couples that light up and burn about as bright as a Roman Candle but fade out nearly as quickly. It's only a slight exaggeration to say that, per romance in the Boy Soi, "tonight you're my boyfriend, tomorrow night my ex." So, while I'm reasonably certain that both Bon and I are excited—turned on, intoxicated even—with our new couple-ness, in these early days I'm also fairly sure that being together in five or ten years isn't crossing our minds. There must be some other factors, other connections beyond sexual intimacy alone, to provide the necessary glue for bonding a real relationship.

I've already mentioned the one other common, connecting factor. One that I believe best enables our transition over time, from casual boyfriends to committed partners. Family ties—respect for and obligation to our individual families. In Thailand, Rule #1 for any foreigner with a young Thai boyfriend is quite simply this: if it comes down to spending time with the foreign guy or fulfilling a family obligation, the family obligation wins out. For Western gays, especially older ones who are "helping out" their younger boyfriends with monthly rent or even send-home-to-family money, this rule rarely sits well. It can even lead to break-ups. As a small, indirect example of what I'm talking about, take Bon's need to—at whatever hour the day or night ends for us—return to his apartment, rather than to instead "move in" to the

Silom Serene (or, eventually, to the condo I will rent) so we can live together for as long as I'm in town each trip.

For the first couple of years that Bon and I are boyfriends, I confess that I yearn for his 24/7 company. To have him sleep with me each night and wake up holding each other in the morning. Sure, there are those few occasions when, too drunk to awaken, he ends up staying until noon the next day. But then, always he returns to his place, and we meet up somewhere later on. Still, the normal routine is come and go. At times, in my often too-sensitive-for-my-own-good moments, the fact that he prefers not to move in hurts to the heart. But I make no demands. How can I, really? I want Bon to *want* to be with me, not to *have* to be with me. Western gays I meet while in Bangkok are typically surprised to hear Bon and I don't stay and sleep together while I'm in Thailand. They sometimes ask, "Why don't you tell him to stay with you?" For me, the answer lies in the question itself: I don't want to **tell** Bon anything. I want us to have a respectful relationship, not some kind of pressured dictatorship.

Back to Rule #1, with an ex-wife and two sons I care much for, I understand the super-priority family can, from time to time, claim. Of course, Bon has his own apartment because he lives and works in Bangkok full-time; and I'm only here, at best, twelve weeks a year. But there's more to it than this. Bon's family—especially his mom, two younger brothers, and close cousins—are in and out of the city, often unannounced. His mom is known to arrive from their home district near Sakon Nakhon at 5 a.m., after an eleven-hour van ride. She ends up knocking on his door, waking him up, and occasionally staying with him in the apartment for a few days. Same with his brothers, Boy and Dam. Even after his family comes to know and like me, Bon needs to maintain some vague pretense. Despite the accepted prevalence of gays and other LGBTQ types throughout all of Thailand, what's not so common is to directly come out and tell your family that you're gay. And Bon has, up to now anyway, never uttered such a thing to anyone in his family. A don't ask don't tell arrangement everyone seems more than okay with.

Fortunately, unlike many of those Westerners who question me about Bon's separate living space, I get all of this. Better still, I eventually get over the hurt heart syndrome of those first few years when I end up sleeping most nights in Bangkok alone. In fact, like Bon, I come to realize and appreciate even that, by not being together every waking or sleeping minute I'm in Thailand *and* by not being together every week or month of the year, we never grow tired of or petty with one another. Virtually each time we reunite, our faces light up again, almost as if meeting for the first time.

There's something else, though, about the importance of family connection to advancing our incipient relationship-building. For starters, I meet and begin assimilating some into the Jaranai Family, Bon's rather large set of immediate and extended relatives. Call it a portal for me into a much deeper relationship with Bon, that first step in my adopting of (or, do I have it backwards?) my being adopted by a second family. That very first visit to his parents' farm home in Northeast Thailand will remain unforgettable with, in my mind anyway, overtones of the destiny Buddha seems to have in store for us.

The occasion of this first visit is spiritual and celebratory—Bon has decided it's his time to become a Buddhist monk. Not for life, mind you. Rather, as I learn, each Thai male is expected to join his local temple *sangha* (community), take instruction, and be ordained as a Buddhist monk; residing thereafter in that community for anywhere from seven to thirty or more days, before returning to his normal life. And, though any Thai adult male may make this spiritual commitment at any time, it is generally hoped, especially by the man's parents, that he will undergo ordination before he turns thirty. It's not possible to overestimate the significance of a young man becoming a monk. Though I'm virtually 100% naïve regarding this significance as I travel with Bon for the very first time to his rural boyhood home, it soon appears evident that becoming a monk is a much bigger deal than, say, a daughter or son's marriage. The experience engenders an enormous amount of pride among fathers and mothers. But even more to be valued, it stores up considerable merit for the young man and his family. And for devout Buddhists, the more the merit in this life, the better the experience in the next.

I could say many things about the three days comprising all the ceremonies—both at Bon's home and at the temple a short walk away. There is also the grand party of a few hundred relatives, neighbors, and various district dignitaries spilling out onto the road from his parent's property. Snapshot moments remain vivid in my memory. One such moment is being asked, along with Bon's grandfather, dad, and three brothers, to clip some of his hair prior to the head monk's shaving of Bon's head. Another is that stoic stone-face Bon sustains once he is ordained: his transformation from cool, sexy, young gay to reverent, prayerful young monk is both real—and, to me, unreal.

But the mini-movie memory that plays most frequently and poignantly to this day records that early morning wake-up, around 5:45 a.m. It was after spending my first night sleeping side-by-side Bon (but politely separate from each other) on the upstairs floor of his home. Before turning in that night, Bon's dad—despite having just met me that afternoon—asks Bon if I'd like to accompany him early the next day to feed the monks. Bon insists that I need not do this if I'm too tired after our long drive from Bangkok. My response, though, is automatic. Since neither his dad, nor anyone in his entire family save one other person, can speak English, I'm looking for *any* way, nonverbal or otherwise, to be better acquainted with Bon's family. So, upon being awakened, I pull on yesterday's shorts and T-shirt, slip into my flip-flops left by the front door, and wait for Bon's dad to meet me on their patio.

Bon's mom provides the "food": sticky rice in its traditional wicker basket, which Bon's dad will form into balls and place into each monk's brass bowl as he passes by. For me, packaged Fun-Oh cookie snacks on a platter to place in the same manner.

We walk no more than ninety meters from the house to join, perhaps, eight or ten mostly elderly neighbors who are already standing and chatting along the dirt road. They, too, each hold a basket of sticky rice. But it's that short walk to join them that I find so telling. Bon's dad is slim, slight, even diminutive. And though he is about seven or eight years younger than me, his long years growing rice and rubber trees in the Thai sun makes him look a good bit older. Like Bon, his smile is large and welcoming. I know he would like conversing with me as much as I would with him, but without any comprehensible words to say, we simply walk and smile. And then it happens, uncontrollably. About halfway to our roadside line-up, I start giggling then end up laughing out loud. Bon's dad, maybe thinking I'm just a happy guy, smiles my way and laughs some too. But, luckily, he cannot read my mind. It's this suddenly ludicrous image coming into focus: here are two older men who just recently laid eyes on each other for the first time. One small, dark-skinned and Esan-Thai. The other tall, snow-white skinned, and undoubtedly the only foreigner within two-hundred kilometers, walking as if lifelong friends side-by-side to feed some Buddhist monks and receive their blessings. But what makes this image so preposterously comedic—both men love the same guy; one as Dad, the other (old enough to be his dad) as Lover. And neither bats an eye.

I savor this simple but singular moment, walking alongside Bon's dad one morning at daybreak in far off rural Thailand. It represents, symbolically, a hopeful transition as a gay man for me. Bon has never told his family that he's gay. But they know. Before introducing me to them, Bon tells his parents about me; that I'm American, older, divorced, and with adult sons. He doesn't tell them I'm gay. But they know. So much unsaid, yet I'm so warmly welcomed into their family. Though I've not lost my own family back home, I have watched it break apart in order for me to become the gay guy I know now, for sure, I am. Becoming part of Bon's family so effortlessly, then, doesn't just bring the two of us closer. It helps me believe that my choice to accept and become gay even this late in my life is, more and more, the right one. And all of this, coincidentally, with Bon wearing the saffron robes of the Buddha.

So, to my way of thinking, the fifteen years Bon and I have now spent growing an ever-evolving, ever-stronger relationship all trace back to these two, effortless, uncomplicated first meetings: the "light touch" ease with which I first meet Bon at Future Boys and the acceptive ease with which I first join his family in the heart of Esan. Of course, during that decade and a half span, there are other significant "family ties" contributing to the success of our improbable partnership. For example, when I finally get Bon to tell me about all three of his brothers. The two younger ones, Boy and Dam, he mentions early and often as we talk through those long nights at Silom Serene. But of his one older brother, Dew, he says little and seems to prefer changing the subject from. Until one night on our condo balcony, after we're boyfriends but before I make that first visit to his home.

I cannot recall exactly how Dew's name comes up that night. I think it's while I'm asking Bon to tell me more about his initial summer-work move to Bangkok, when he was still a teenager and bussing tables at a restaurant where Dew also worked as a bartender. Bon interrupts me. He says something like, "Mike, I need to tell you about my brother, Dew. I hope it won't upset you." I stare back at him, saying nothing at first, unable to imagine what in the world Bon might tell me about Dew that would upset me. Is he into drugs? Some kind of criminal background? Then Bon says, "Dew is *gatoey*." That would be Thai for ladyboy, in today's LGBTQ parlance, transgender. My stare morphs into smile as I simply reply, "Oh, that's all. Okay by me."

Although we have since reminisced and laughed about this moment a few times, I'm still not sure why Bon thought I might be upset to learn that, not only is he, the second son in the family, gay, but the first son in the family also happens to be trans. That would be two "not-so-normal" sons in a row. Embarrassment? Maybe a bit.

It's not exactly the run-of-the-mill family, is it? But even though I've never met any transgender types, I have absolutely no problem with them. How could I? I thought I was and pretended to be straight for fifty years; now I'm gay. As Pope Francis would say, "Who am I to judge?"

So, not long after this balcony admission, I ask to meet Dew, who is living and working as a stylist at a Bangkok salon. I love Dew from the start, and he instantly becomes like a brother—or is it sister? Sister-in-law?—to me. In fact, as my first-ever transgender close friend (and relative), Dew introduces me to the many other *gatoeys* he knows, both in Bangkok and at home in Esan, for which I become ever grateful. Of the many, many nights Bon and I enjoy bar-hopping the sois of Silom, none are as fun, funny, crazy, or memorable as the ones with our ladyboy friends. As I've come to learn and appreciate so much, in their shared not-normalness, gays and *gatoeys* go together naturally like whiskey and soda, not surprisingly the favorite social drink of both.

Aside from becoming Bon's partner and a member of his Esan family, there remains one other missing link for my complete transition from straight married American guy to gay husband Thai guy. Bon must get to know my family—my sons anyway—as I've come to know his. So when my younger son tells me that he and his wife want to visit me while I'm in Thailand, I'm thrilled. Both sons know by now that I have some kind of gay life in Bangkok, though neither has asked about it, nor have I risked burdening them with too much information. But, as one of my sons will now be joining me in Bangkok, it's time for a little background. Over a burger a week or so before we all begin travels westward, I tell my son that I have a Thai significant other whom, of course, I want him to meet. I talk about how my friend's personality is so alike his and his brother's—quiet, soft-spoken, non-contentious, and kind-hearted. I also speak some of Bon's family and how much I care for them, and they for me. Only one thing I, for the time being, leave out: that my significant other/friend is only twenty-four, which means he's roughly six years younger than my son. I figure I'll mention this minor detail once he and his wife arrive in Thailand.

If I have any butterflies inside while awaiting my son's and his wife's first visit to Bangkok, they dissipate almost immediately. I have booked a hotel for the two of them on Silom Road within walking distance of my condo. Once I know they've checked in, I meet up with them in their lobby and walk them to the place Bon and I now share in lieu of Silom Serene. Bon will join us here in an hour or so, but first I want them to see my Thai home, where I plan to share some framed photos—of me with Bon. As I hand down one of the pictures I like best, I say, "Here's Bon. He's twenty-four, by the way. I guess you can say he's my *boy* . . . friend?" At which, both my son and his wife laugh out loud. Their natural reaction makes everything crystal clear: meeting Bon is going to go fine, as will our times together. And they do. In fact, within another two years, the four of us will travel to Shanghai, Beijing and the Great Wall, as well as take a forty-four hour train ride from Beijing to Lhasa, in Tibet—a train on which we will share a berth with six bunks, four for us and two for a young Chinese couple. Finally, I'm not just part of Bon's family; he's also part of mine.

There's this billboard, you can't miss it, above a PrEP shop conveniently gay-located on Silom Road. Bon and I see it one day as we cross over Silom through the BTS-Skytrain station, which is always the safest way to circumvent the insane, gridlocked traffic below. The billboard aims to advertise HIV and STD preventive supplements and various other treatments available within the shop. We've no interest in the shop or its products, but the words on the sign speak to us both: *"Be gay. It's OK."* Makes us laugh as we pass it by, the rhyming and the goofy message it conveys. A slogan for two guys, together now just over fifteen years that rings so true. Our gay years have been OK—and then some. Descending the stairs from the BTS platform to the other side of Silom (that would be the side leading to our favorite gay sois and bars), I'm thinking—it's a helluva lot more than just OK. For me, after all the disbeliefs, denials, delays, and doubts, "Be Gay" is nothing less than the right choice.

AFTERWORD

"Same, same. But different."

A good friend who knew I was writing a book asked me, "What kind of book is it?" I answered, "It's not an autobiography. It's not a memoir. It's not a confessional (though, funnily enough, it does include an episode dealing with a Confession). It's more a story of self-discovery." As I reread this story of mine, from back then to now, I ask, "What, then, of relevance—to me or anyone else—have I discovered about myself?"

It would not be unfair to conclude that a good part of my self-discovery is not all that, shall we say, flattering. First of all, there are those lies. While I do not claim to have lived my life without bending the truth occasionally on inconsequential matters, these lies to cover up my shame (with Father Tom) and my gayness (with my wife) can in no way be considered inconsequential. Why spin them, when so out of character? The answer seems rather simple. You don't have to be in the public eye with big reputations or big money at stake—as with celebrities, politicians, clergy—all the while staring at an unmasking that could undo everything. The basic human impulse, nine point nine times of out ten, is to lie. But fortunately, for me anyway, despite my attempt at merely buying some time delaying the inevitable, I discovered rather quickly that the truth always will out. More than this, regardless of the immediate pain, I wholeheartedly buy into that oft-quoted university slogan—"the truth shall set you free." It sure has for me.

Then there's that equally unflattering immaturity—or is it gullibility (or both)—that I exhibited so routinely in my rush to discover or somehow prove my gayness to myself. From online escort service to gay massage club to Boy Soi bar, my behaviors usually seemed much more those of a pubescent teen than of a fifty-plus, well-adjusted adult. And throughout the many wild nights out with Joe and his buds or Bon and his fellow Future Boys, so often paying everyone and for everything in sight, was I patently seeking appreciation? Wanting desperately to be liked despite my age? No doubt I spent many days pretending to be a young guy again, as well as trying in some way to compensate for (in truth) lost youth, lost sexual attraction. I've also already stated that I offer little in defense of these behaviors.

Thankfully, throughout all of this, I learned something super-important about myself. Namely, I'm the kind of person who *needs* to help someone, to take care of someone. Perhaps it's a little like Bon's need to help his parents, to take care of his parents as much as he can—for his own self-esteem. The same holds true for me. When I was helping Joe and his family or when I'm now helping Bon and his family, it's in large part for my own self-esteem. Then, too, I also discovered that being routinely, consistently kind—jai di in Thai—is a much more potent form of sexual attraction than I ever imagined. My strategy of "smothering with kindness" not only came rather easily to me, but it worked. How do I know? Bon tells me so all the time. Even should I, out of the blue, ask him why he fell for me, I always get the same answer: "Mike, I never met any guy as kind as you."

Beyond these character flaws, however, my tale of self-discovery has gifted me with two eye-opening insights. One physical-psychological and the other spiritual. First, there's Joseph's sexual orientation continuum, which having lived through, I know to be reality and not theory. In my many discussions with Joseph about my sexual attractions and desires—from early teen years through young adulthood to approaching senior-hood—nothing is clearer to me now than my own gravitation from, most likely, bisexual teen to middle-aged gay. As I detailed my middle school, high school, and college years and acquaintances to him, I could see it plainly. That while I dreamed of finding a girl to love me and to marry, I also ached at times for an intimacy with boys and young guys my own age. Of course, in those days, I simply assumed such dual attractions were "normal." The continuum is real. I've lived it. Felt myself moving along it. And though I cannot precisely say what triggers along the line pushed me further left to my ultimate gayness, I'm pretty sure the voice in my head as I turned fifty was one of them: "If you don't act now, find out now, you'll be way too old and it will be way too late to ever find a loving, gay relationship." A twist on that age-old expression, "act now or for never be at peace."

As to the more spiritual insight I've alluded to, much derives from being with and loving a young devout Buddhist guy all these years. I had a passing interest in Buddhism before I ever entered Thailand. My familiarity with the beloved Vietnamese monk, Thich Nhat Hanh, and especially his book *Living Buddha, Living Christ*, first piqued my interest. It led to my discovering just how closely aligned were the teachings, the Way of Living Rightly, of Buddha and Jesus. But it was only reading and some light thinking—until I met Bon and began learning more from him and his family. They showed me just how seamlessly Buddhism beliefs intertwine with daily life among devout Thai's. Thailand happens to be the most populous Buddhist country in the world, with roughly 95% of Thai's professing to be Buddhist. Thailand also happens to be—and has been for as long as anyone can remember—the most gay-friendly, gay-accepting country in the world. These two mosts are not coincidental.

Buddhists, adhering to so many of the same life's principles as Christians, believe you must be true to who you are. And, providing who you are is kind, compassionate, and averse to harming any other creature, nothing else matters. Believing and living this way not only makes imminent sense to me, it just feels right. So right that, after sharing so much of my life with a good and committed Buddhist, when people occasionally ask me what religion I follow, I now reply, "Buddo-Christian."

Within a duo-spiritual framework such as this, I consider again that intentionally provocative word in my title, *choosing*. Christians and Buddhists alike adhere to a belief in free will. And yet, most Christians also believe that, while their will to choose—right/wrong, good/bad—is ultimately theirs, through faith and prayer, the Lord guides them, shows them the Way. In a not so different sense, Buddhist's who live according to the Buddha's Eightfold Path don't merely find a means to end suffering, they also find the Right Way. My odyssey from living straight to loving gay is so ironic and improbable that I'm certain I've also been guided. Ironic in that, after living straight for so long, I unwittingly choose a straight guy (and married!) as my first gay love; improbable in that this same straight guy inadvertently but fortuitously introduces me to my life's gay partner. Surely, there must be some guiding behind my choosing. Which makes me reconsider that title one last time. Perhaps not *Choosing To Be Gay*, but better stated, *Chosen To Be Gay*.

In T-shirt crazed Bangkok, there's another one I've long had my eyes on. On the shirt's front read those two oddest but most common English words Thai's use when talking with foreigners, "Same, same." And on the back, this follow-up punchline: "But different." After all my years in Bangkok, I freely admit I have no idea about the origins of "same, same." I just know I've heard it uttered more times than I can count—usually in casual conversation between a Westerner and a Thai, agreeing about something in common each has experienced. Looking back now over the up and down episodes of my story, these T-shirt embossed words take on another relevant meaning for me—and I hope, for others.

Perhaps you are twelve years old and aimlessly trying to figure out how to come out to your parents, siblings, and friends. Or perhaps you are more like me, years into a virtually straight adult life and trying to figure out how at this late date you got here. It doesn't matter. The voices in your head, those urging you to disbelieve, deny, or doubt who you truly are speak to each of us. The personalities and situations we each encounter may be different, but the daunting ultimate choice to accept and become oneself is always the same. And, being so daunting, it's a choice that once made and pursued to the fullest, deserves everyone's acceptance, and respect.

www.ingramcontent.com/pod-product-compliance
Lightning Source LLC
Chambersburg PA
CBHW032123090426
42743CB00007B/434